Somehow Form
a Family

Also by Tony Earley

Here We Are in Paradise, a collection of stories
Jim the Boy, a novel

SOMEHOW
FORM
A FAMILY

Stories That Are Mostly True

TONY EARLEY

A SHANNON RAVENEL BOOK

Algonquin Books of Chapel Hill   2002

A SHANNON RAVENEL BOOK

Published by
ALGONQUIN BOOKS OF CHAPEL HILL
Post Office Box 2225
Chapel Hill, North Carolina 27515-2225

a division of
Workman Publishing
708 Broadway
New York, New York 10003

In several of these essays, some names have been changed
to protect the innocent and/or the guilty.

Library of Congress Cataloging-in-Publication Data
Earley, Tony, 1961–
    Somehow form a family : stories that are mostly true /
Tony Earley.
        p. cm.
    "A Shannon Ravenel book"—T.p. verso.
    ISBN 1-56512-302-6
    1. Earley, Tony, 1961—Childhood and youth.   2. Earley,
Tony, 1961—Homes and haunts—North Carolina.
    3. Novelists, American—20th century—Biography.
    4. North Carolina—Social life and customs.   5. Mountain
life—North Carolina.   6. Family—North Carolina.
    I. Title.
PS3555.A685 Z475 2001
813'.54—dc21
    [B]   00-069452

ISBN 1-56512-360-3 paper
10   9   8   7   6   5   4   3   2   1

For S.C.B.E.

—⚋—

In all that Sarah has said unto thee,
hearken to her voice.

[ACKNOWLEDGMENTS]

NINE OF THE pieces contained in this volume appeared previously in the following magazines: *Harper's*—"Somehow Form a Family" and "Tour de Fax"; the *New Yorker*—"The Quare Gene" and "Granny's Bridge"; the *Oxford American*—"Deer Season, 1974," "Shooting the Cat," "The Courting Garden," "Ghost Stories" (which appeared in the magazine under the title "Ghosts in the Mist"), and "A Worn Path."

"Hallway" first appeared in *Home: American Writers Remember Rooms of Their Own*, edited by Sharon Sloan Fiffer and Steve Fiffer and published by Pantheon Books of New York in 1995.

The author would like to thank Colin Harrison of *Harper's*, Deborah Treisman of the *New Yorker*, and Marc Smirnoff of the *Oxford American* for their encouragement.

This book would not have been written without the unwavering support of Gordon Kato and the grace, wisdom, and patience of Sarah Bell Earley.

[CONTENTS]

—⚹—

"The writer has attempted to write an absolutely true book to see whether the shape of a country and the pattern of a month's action can, if truly presented, compete with a work of the imagination."

—ERNEST HEMINGWAY,
Green Hills of Africa

—◊—

"What's the trouble now? . . . He thinks he can write a piece about anything and get away with it . . . But it isn't the hot stuff he says he knows it is."

— T. S. MATTHEWS
on *Green Hills of Africa*

[INTRODUCTION]

ON THE NIGHT of July 20, 1969, my little sister and I followed our father into the backyard, where we studied the moon through a surveyor's transit owned by a neighbor. Peering through the eyepiece, I felt as if I could almost see Neil Armstrong on the lunar surface, which made the universe seem very large and, simultaneously, very small. It's one of the most vivid memories of my childhood. When I wrote about that night almost thirty years later, I described the full moon in detail, how, once magnified, it had seemed almost too bright to look at. When a fact checker at *Harper's* magazine informed me that the moon on the night of July 20, 1969, had not been full, but had been a waxing crescent, I refused at first to believe her. When I looked it up for myself and discovered that she was right, I was faced on one hand with a memory so strong I was sure it had to be true, and on the other hand with an objective truth significantly different than what I remembered. At that moment I came to understand, if not embrace, the true nature of the phrase *creative nonfiction.*

When I remember that night, the moon I see in my mind's eye is still full; that the moon was, in fact, a waxing crescent relegates what I remember to the realm of fiction, the mysterious land of story, where any fact can be abandoned if a writer finds it inconvenient enough. But even if I had remembered the phase of the moon correctly, the resulting personal essay would have been only marginally more deserving of the tag *nonfiction,* while remaining as "creative" as it had been while the imaginary moon floating over North Carolina remained full. As a writer, every time I place the boy I was thirty-one years ago in that particular backyard, staring up at that particular sky, I am, in effect, conjuring him—making myself up—as much as I would any "fictional" character. Memory and imagination seem to me the same human property, known by different names. Clark Kent and Superman are, after all, the same muscular guy; the only difference between them lies in how they are packaged and perceived.

While it is necessary for our sanity to keep the line between fiction and nonfiction clearly drawn, that particular boundary, as with the boundaries between nations, is more arbitrary than we might care to think. Good novels and short stories are most often praised as "true" by critics, while successful memoirs are invariably compared to novels. The personal essayist recounting a conversation he participated in twenty-five years ago (as I do several times in this book), and the short story writer making up a conversation between fictional characters are basically engaged in the same exercise. Both are taking subjective human experience and converting it into narrative.

The narrative form—a story with a beginning, middle, and end—is not only a way for us to relate information about the universe to each other, but a reflection of the universe itself. Both the big bang theory and the story of creation in Genesis share the narrative form; both the physicist and the theologian give this biggest story of all a beginning and middle, as well as a promised end. We are born, live, and die; the sun rises and sets; every small stream runs downhill to the sea. The stars and planets in their intricate spinning tell the same story day after day; meanwhile the galaxies fly at unimaginable speed away from the initial spark of their creation, toward an inevitable end. Nothing in the physical world—time nor distance, and certainly not the personal essay—is inseparable from the narrative mind of God.

This book is a collection of personal essays, although I call it that simply because I didn't know what else to call it. I hesitate to use the designation *personal* because it has come to suggest, with some justification, a certain contemporary predisposition toward narcissism. And I hesitate to call the ten pieces collected here essays because only one of them, "The Quare Gene," strikes me as an essay in what I came to understand years ago as the essay form. At its heart this book is a collection of stories. I say that they are mostly true because memory, like imagination, is largely a function of individual perception. The other people involved in these essays/stories will no doubt remember the events described here differently because it would be impossible for them to do otherwise.

The great irony of the personal essay is that the essayist attempts to illuminate universal human truths by talking about himself, in much the same way a basketball player jumps by pushing his feet into the floor, a counterintuitive proposition at best. The only way that the word *personal* can be made more noxious is to immediately follow it with the word *journey,* but again, for lack of a better phrase, this book is an account of just such a trip. It's the story of how I started out at one place and ended up at another, making myself up as I went along. Rewriting oneself on the fly seems to me a basic human—and particularly American—avocation. To that end, I offer this book as a representative account, and my sincerest hope is that readers will be able to recognize themselves in its pages.

[Somehow Form a Family]

In July 1969, I looked a lot like Opie in the second or third season of *The Andy Griffith Show*. I was a small boy with a big head. I wore blue jeans with the cuffs turned up and horizontally striped pullover shirts. I was the brother in a father-mother-brother-sister family. We lived in a four-room house at the edge of the country, at the foot of the mountains, outside a small town in North Carolina, but it could have been anywhere.

On one side of us lived Mr. and Mrs. White. They were old and rich. Their driveway was paved. Mrs. White was the president of the town garden club. When she came to visit Mama she brought her own ashtray. Mr. White was almost deaf. When he watched the news on television, it sounded like thunder in the distance. The Whites had an aluminum travel trailer in which you could see your reflection. One summer they hitched it to their Chrysler and pulled it all the way to Alaska.

On the other side of us lived Mack and Joan. They had just graduated from college. I thought Joan was beautiful, and still do. Mack had a bass boat and a three-tray tackle box in which lurked a bristling school of lures. On the other side of Mack and Joan lived Mrs. Taylor, who was old, and on the other side of Mrs. Taylor lived Mr. and Mrs. Frady, who had a fierce dog. My sister, Shelly, and I called it the Frady dog. The Frady dog lived a long and bitter life. It did not die until well after I had a driver's license.

On the far side of the Whites lived Mr. and Mrs. John Harris; Mr. and Mrs. Burlon Harris lived beyond them. John and Burlon were first cousins. John was a teacher who in the summers fixed lawn mowers, including ours, in a building behind his house. Burlon reminded me of Mr. Greenjeans on *Captain Kangaroo*. He kept horses and let us play in his barn. Shelly once commandeered one of his cats and brought it home to live with us. Burlon did not mind; he asked her if she wanted another one. We rode our bicycles toward Mr. Harris's house as if pulled there by gravity. We did not ride in the other direction; the Frady dog sat in its yard and watched for us.

In July 1969, we did not have much money, but in the hi-
erarchy of southern poor, we were the good kind, the kind
you would not mind living on your road. We were clean. Our
clothes were clean. My parents worked. We went to church.
Easter mornings, Mama stood us in front of the yellowbell
bush and took our picture. We had meat at every meal—
chicken and cube steak and pork chops and ham—and
plenty of milk to drink. We were not trashy. Mrs. White would
not sit with her ashtray in the kitchen of trashy people. Trashy
people lived in the two houses around the curve past Mr.
Harris's. When Daddy drove by those houses we could see
that the kids in the yard had dirty faces. They were usually
jabbing at something with a stick. Shelly and I were not allowed to ride our bicycles around the curve.

I knew we were poor only because our television was black
and white. It was an old Admiral, built in the 1950s, with brass
knobs the size of baseballs. Its cabinet was perfectly square, a
cube of steel with a painted-on mahogany grain. Hoss on
Bonanza could not have picked it up by himself. It was a for-
midable object, but its vertical hold was shot. We gathered
around it the night Neil Armstrong walked on the moon, but
we could not tell what was happening. The picture flipped
up and down. We turned off the lights in the living room so
we could see better. We listened to Walter Cronkite. In the
distance we could hear Mr. White's color TV rumbling. We

changed the channel and listened to Huntley and Brinkley. We could hear the scratchy radio transmissions coming down out of space, but we could not see anything. Daddy got behind the TV with a flashlight. He said, "Is that better? Is that better?" but it never was. Mama said, "Just be thankful you've got a television."

After the Eagle had landed but before the astronauts opened the door and came out, Mack knocked on the door and asked us if we wanted to look at the moon. He was an engineer for a power company and had set up his surveyor's transit in the backyard. Daddy and Shelly and I went with him. We left Mama sitting in the living room in the blue light of the TV. She said she did not want to miss anything. The moon, as I remember it, was full, although I have since learned that it wasn't. I remember that a galaxy of lightning bugs blinked against the black pine trees that grew between our yard and that of the Whites. Mack pointed the transit at the sky. Daddy held me up so I could see. The moon inside the instrument was startlingly bright; the man in the moon was clearly visible, although the men on the moon weren't. "You can't see them or anything," Mack said, which I already knew. I said, "I know that." I wasn't stupid and did not like to be talked to as if I were. Daddy put me down. He and Mack stood for a while and talked. Daddy smoked a cigarette. In the bright yard Shelly chased lightning bugs. She did not run, but instead jumped slowly, her feet together. I realized that she was pretending to walk on the moon, pretending that she was weightless. The moon was so bright, it cast a shadow at her feet. I remember these things for sure. I am tempted to say that she was beautiful in the moonlight, and I'm sure she was, but that isn't something I remember noticing that night, only a thing I need to say now.

—⁂—

EIGHT, MAYBE nine months later, Shelly and I rode the bus home from school. It was a Thursday, Mama's day off, Easter time. The cherry tree in the garden separating our driveway from that of the Whites was in brilliant, full bloom. We could hear it buzzing from the road. One of us checked the mailbox. We looked up the driveway at our house. Something was wrong with it, but we couldn't tell what. Daddy was adding four rooms on to the house, and we were used to it appearing large and unfinished. We stood in the driveway and stared. Black tar paper was tacked to the outside walls of the new part, but the old part was still covered with white asbestos shingles. In the coming summer, Daddy and a crew of brick masons would finish transforming the house into a split-level ranch style, remarkably similar to the one in which the Bradys would live. I loved the words *split-level ranch-style*. To me they meant "rich."

Shelly and I spotted what was wrong at the same time. A giant television antenna had attached itself to the roof of our house. It was shiny and tall as a young tree. It looked dangerous, as if it would bite, like a praying mantis. The antenna slowly began to turn, as if it had noticed us. Shelly and I looked quickly at each other, our mouths wide open, and then back at the antenna. We sprinted up the driveway.

In the living room, on the spot occupied by the Admiral that morning, sat a magnificent new color TV, a Zenith, with a twenty-one-inch screen. Its cabinet was made of real wood. *Gomer Pyle, U.S.M.C.* was on. I will never forget that. Gomer Pyle and Sergeant Carter were the first two people I ever saw on a color television. The olive green and khaki of their uniforms was dazzling. Above them was the blue sky of California. The sky in California seemed bluer than the sky in North Carolina.

We said, "Is that ours?"

Mama said, "I'm going to kill your daddy." He had charged the TV without telling her. Two men from Sterchi's Furniture had showed up at the house that morning with the TV on a truck. They climbed onto the roof and planted the antenna.

We said, "Can we keep it?"

Mama said, "I don't know," but I noticed she had written the numbers of the stations we could get on the dial of the Channel Master, the small box which controlled the direction the antenna pointed. Mama would never have written on anything she planned on taking back to the store.

The dial of the Channel Master was marked like a compass. Channel 3 in Charlotte lay to the east; Channel 13 in Asheville lay to the west. Channel 7 in Spartanburg and Channel 4 in Greenville rested side by side below them in the south. For years these cities would mark the outside edges of the world as I knew it. Shelly reached out and turned the dial. Mama smacked her on the hand. Gomer grew fuzzy and disappeared. I said, "Mama, she broke it." When the dial stopped turning, Mama carefully turned it back to the south. Gomer reappeared, resurrected. Jim Nabors probably never looked better to anyone, in his whole life, than he did to us right then.

Mama sat us down on the couch and laid down the law. Mama always laid down the law when she was upset. We were not to touch the TV. We could not turn it on, nor could we change the channel. Under no circumstances were we to touch the Channel Master. The Channel Master was very expensive. And if we so much as looked at the knobs that controlled the color, she would whip us. It had taken her all afternoon to get the color just right.

—⚏—

WE LIVED in a split-level ranch-style house, with two maple trees and a rose bush in the front yard, outside a town that could have been named Springfield. We had a color TV. We had a Channel Master antenna that turned slowly on top of our house until it found and pulled from the sky electromagnetic waves for our nuclear family.

We watched *Hee-Haw*, starring Buck Owens and Roy Clark; we watched *All in the Family*, *The Mary Tyler Moore Show*, *The Bob Newhart Show*, *The Carol Burnett Show*, and *Mannix*, starring Mike Connors with Gail Fisher as Peggy; we watched *Gunsmoke* and *Bonanza*, even after Adam left and Hoss died and Little Joe's hair turned gray; we watched *Adam-12* and *Kojak*, *McCloud*, *Colombo*, and *Hawaii Five-O*; we watched *Cannon*, a Quinn Martin production and *Barnaby Jones*, a Quinn Martin production, which co-starred Miss America and Uncle Jed from *The Beverly Hillbillies*. Daddy finished the new part of the house and moved out soon thereafter. He rented a trailer in town and took the old Admiral out of the basement with him. We watched *Mutual of Omaha's Wild Kingdom* and *The Wonderful World of Disney*. After school we watched *Gomer Pyle, U.S.M.C.*, *The Beverly Hillbillies*, *Gilligan's Island*, and *The Andy Griffith Show*. Upstairs, we had rooms of our own. Mama stopped taking us to church.

On Friday nights we watched *The Partridge Family*, *The Brady Bunch*, *Room 222*, *The Odd Couple*, and *Love American Style*. Daddy came to visit on Saturdays. We watched *The*

Little Rascals on Channel 3 with Fred Kirby, the singing cowboy, and his sidekick, Uncle Jim. We watched *The Little Rascals* on Channel 4 with Monty Dupuy, the weatherman, and his sidekick, Doohickey. Mornings, before school, we watched *The Three Stooges* with Mr. Bill on Channel 13. Mr. Bill worked alone. The school year Daddy moved out, Mr. Bill showed Bible story cartoons instead of *The Three Stooges*. That year, we went to school angry.

After each of Daddy's visits, Mama said he was getting better. Shelly and I tried to imagine living with the Bradys but realized we would not fit in. They were richer and more popular at school. They did not have Southern accents. One Saturday Daddy brought me a set of golf clubs, which I had asked for but did not expect to get. It was raining that day. I took the clubs out in the yard and very quickly realized that golf was harder than it looked on television. I went back inside and wiped the mud and water off the clubs with Bounty paper towels, the quicker picker upper. Upstairs I heard Mama say, "Do you think he's stupid?" I spread the golf clubs on the floor around me. I tuned in *Shock Theater* on Channel 13 and turned it up loud.

Shelly had a crush on Bobby Brady; I had a crush on Jan. Jan had braces, I had braces. Jan had glasses, I had glasses. Their daddy was an architect. Our daddy lived in a trailer in town with a poster of Wile E. Coyote and the Road Runner on the living room wall. The Coyote held the Road Runner firmly by the neck. The caption on the poster said, "Beep, Beep your ass." I lay in bed at night and imagined being married to Jan Brady but having an affair with Marsha. I wondered how we would tell Jan, what Marsha and I would do then, where we would go. Greg Brady beat me up. I shook his hand and told him I deserved it. Alice refused to speak to me. During this time Mrs. White died. I heard the ambulance in the middle of the night. It sounded like the one on *Emergency*. I opened the door to Mama's room to see if she was OK. She was embarrassed because our dog barked and barked.

Rhoda left *The Mary Tyler Moore Show*. Maude and George Jefferson left *All in the Family*; Florida, Maude's maid, left *Maude*. Daddy moved back in. He watched the news during supper, the TV as loud as Mr. White's. We were not allowed to talk during the news. This was the law. After the news we watched *Rhoda* or *Maude* or *Good Times*. Daddy decided that cutting the grass should be my job. We had a big yard. I decided that I didn't want to do anything he said. Mr. White remarried. The new Mrs. White's daughter died of cancer. The new Mrs. White dug up every flower the old Mrs. White had planted; she cut down every tree and shrub, including the cherry tree in the garden between our driveways. Mama said the new Mrs. White broke her heart. Mr. White mowed and mowed and mowed their grass until it was smooth as a golf course. Mack and Joan paved their driveway.

What I'm trying to say is this: we lived in a split-level ranch-style house; we had a Zenith in the living room and a Channel Master attached to the roof. But Shelly and I fought like Thelma and J.J. on *Good Times*. I wanted to live in Hawaii and work for Steve McGarrett. No bad guy ever got away from McGarrett, except the Chinese master spy Wo Fat. Shelly said McGarrett would never give me a job. In all things Shelly was on Daddy's side; I lined up on Mama's. Friday evenings, when Daddy got home from work, I sneaked outside to snoop around in the glove compartment of his car. I pretended I had a search warrant, that I was Danno on a big case. Shelly reported my snooping to Daddy. I was trying to be a good son.

Every Saturday, before he went to work, Daddy left word that I was to cut the grass before he got home. I stayed in bed until lunch. Shelly came into my room and said, "You better get up." I flipped her the bird. She said, "I'm telling." I got up in time to watch professional wrestling on Channel 3. I hated the bad guys. They did not fight fair. They hid brass knuckles in their trunks and beat the good guys until they bled. They won too often. Mama brought me tomato and onion sandwiches. I could hear Mack on one side and Mr. White on the other mowing their grass. I could hear John Harris and

Mr. Frady and Mrs. Taylor's daughter, Lucille, mowing grass. Lucille lived in Charlotte, but came home on weekends just to mow Mrs. Taylor's grass. We had the shaggiest lawn on the road. After wrestling, I watched the *Game of the Week* on Channel 4. Carl Yastrzemski of the Boston Red Sox was my favorite baseball player. He had forearms like fenceposts. Nobody messed with him. I listened over the lawn mowers for the sound of Daddy's Volkswagen. Mama came in the living room and said, "Son, maybe you should mow some of the grass before your daddy gets home. You know what's going to happen." I knew what was going to happen. I knew that eventually he would make me mow the grass. I knew that when I was through, Mack would come through the pine trees laughing. He would say, "Charles, I swear that is the laziest boy I have ever seen." Mack had a Snapper Comet riding mower, on which he sat like a king. I never saw him on it that I did not want to bean him with a rock. Daddy would shake his head and say, "Mack, dead lice wouldn't fall off that boy." Every Saturday night we ate out at Scoggin's Seafood and Steak House. *Hee-Haw* came on at seven; *All in the Family* came on at eight.

—⁂—

AND THEN Shelly and I were in high school. We watched *M*A*S*H** and *Lou Grant, Love Boat* and *Fantasy Island*. We watched *Dynasty* and *Dallas*. Opie was Richie Cunningham on *Happy Days*. Ben Cartwright showed up in a black bathrobe on *Battlestar Gallactica*. The Channel Master stopped working, but no one bothered to have it fixed. The antenna was left immobile on the roof in a compromised position: we could almost get most of the channels. One summer Mack built a pool in his backyard. Joan lay in a bikini beside the pool in the sun. The next summer Mack built a fence. This was during the late seventies. Shelly lay in her room with the lights turned off and listened to *Dark Side of the Moon*. On Friday nights she asked me to go out with her and her friends. I always said no. I did not want to miss *The Rockford Files*.

In those days Shelly and I watched *Guiding Light* when we got home from school. It was our soap. I remember that Ed Bauer's beautiful wife Rita left him because he was boring. Shelly said I reminded her of Ed Bauer. She wore her hair like Farrah Fawcett Majors on *Charlie's Angels*. After *Guiding Light* I changed the channel and watched *Star Trek*. I could not stay awake in school. I went to sleep during homeroom. During the day I woke up only long enough to change classes and eat lunch. I watched *Star Trek* when I got home as if it were beamed to our house by God. I did not want to be Captain Kirk, or any of the main characters. I just wanted to go with them. I wanted to wear a red jersey and walk the long, anonymous halls of the Starship Enterprise as it disappeared into space. One day *Star Trek* was preempted by an *ABC After*

School Special. I tried to kick the screen out of the TV. I was wearing sneakers, so the glass would not break. Shelly hid in Mama and Daddy's room. I said, "Five-O. Open up." Then I kicked the door off the hinges.

Our family doctor thought I had narcolepsy. He sent me to a neurologist in Charlotte. Mama and Daddy went with me. In Charlotte, an EEG technician attached wires to my head. A small, round amber light glowed high up in the corner of the examination room. I watched the light until I went to sleep. The neurologist said that the EEG looked normal, but that he would talk to us more about the results in a few minutes. He led us to a private waiting room. It was small and bare and paneled with wood. In it were four chairs. Most of one wall was taken up by a darkened glass. I could not see what was on the other side of it. I studied our reflection. Mama and Daddy were trying to pretend that the glass wasn't there. I said, "Pa, when we get back to the Ponderosa, do you want me to round up those steers on the lower forty?"

Daddy said, "What?"

I said, "Damnit, Jim. I'm a doctor."

Daddy said, "What are you talking about?"

Mama said, "Be quiet. They're watching us."

—⚉—

SHELLY DIED on Christmas Eve morning when I was a freshman in college. She had wrecked Mama's car. That night I stayed up late and watched the Pope deliver the Christmas mass from the Vatican. There was nothing else on. Daddy moved out again. My college almost shut down during the week *The Thorn Birds* was broadcast. Professors rescheduled papers and exams. In the basement of my dorm twenty-five nineteen-year-old guys shouted at the TV when the Richard Chamberlain character told the Rachel Ward character he loved God more than he loved her. At age nineteen, it was impossible to love God more than Rachel Ward. My best friend, a guy from Kenya, talked me into switching from *Guiding Light* to *General Hospital.* This was during the glory days of *General Hospital* when Luke and Scorpio roomed together on the Haunted Star. Laura was supposedly dead, but Luke knew in his heart she was still alive; every time he was by himself he heard a Christopher Cross song.

Going home was strange, as if the Mayberry I expected had become Mayberry, R.F.D. Shelly was gone. Daddy was gone. The second Mrs. White died, then Mr. White went away to a nursing home. The Fradys had moved away. John Harris had a heart attack and stopped fixing lawn mowers. Mama mowed our grass by herself with a rider. I stopped going to see Burlon Harris because he teared up every time he tried to talk about Shelly. Mack and Joan had a son named Timmy. Mack and Joan got a divorce. Mack moved to a farm out in the country; Joan moved to town.

Daddy fell in love with Mama my senior year and moved

back in. The Zenith began slowly dying. Its picture narrowed into a greenly tinted slit. It stared like a diseased eye into the living room where Mama and Daddy sat. They turned off the lights so they could see better. I became a newspaper reporter. With my first Christmas bonus, I bought myself a television, a nineteen-inch GE. With my second Christmas bonus I bought Mama and Daddy one. They hooked it up to cable. When I visited them on Thursdays we watched *The Cosby Show, Family Ties, Cheers, Night Court,* and *Hill Street Blues.* Daddy gave up on broadcast TV when NBC cancelled *Hill Street Blues* and replaced it with *L.A. Law.* Now he mostly watches the Discovery Channel. Mama calls it the "airplanes and animals channel." They are in the eighteenth year of their new life together. I bear them no grudges. They were very young when I knew them best.

In grad school I switched back to *Guiding Light.* I had known Ed Bauer longer than I had known all but a few of my friends. It pleased me to see him in Springfield every afternoon, trying to do good. I watched *The Andy Griffith Show* twice a day. I could glance at Opie and tell you what year the episode was filmed. I watched the Gulf War from a stool in a bar.

Eventually I married a woman who grew up in a family that watched television only on special occasions—when Billie Jean King played Bobby Riggs, when Diana married

Prince Charles. My wife was a student in a seminary. She did not want to meet Ed Bauer, nor could I explain, without sounding pathetic, why Ed Bauer was important to me. The first winter we were married I watched the winter Olympics huddled beneath a blanket in the frigid basement of the house we had rented. This was in a closed-down steel town near Pittsburgh, during the time I contemplated jumping from a bridge into the Ohio River. My wife asked the seminary community to pray for me. Ann B. Davis, who played Alice on *The Brady Bunch* was a member of that community. One day I saw her in the cafeteria at school. She looked much the same as when she played Alice, except that her hair was white, and she wore small, gold glasses. I didn't talk to her. I had heard that she didn't like talking about *The Brady Bunch,* and I could not think of anything to say to her about the world in which we actually lived. I sat in the cafeteria and stared at her as much as I could without anyone noticing. I don't know if she prayed for me or not, but I like to think that she did. I wanted to tell her that I grew up in a split-level ranch-style house outside a small town that could have been named Springfield, but that something had gone wrong inside it. I wanted to tell her that years ago Alice had been important to me, that my sister and I had looked to Alice for something we could not name, and had at least seen a picture of what love looked like. I wanted to tell her that no one in my family ever raised their voice while the television was on, that late at night even a bad television show could keep me from hearing the silence inside my own heart. I wanted to tell her that Ed Bauer and I were still alive, that both of us had always wanted to do what was right. Ann B. Davis stood, walked over to the trash can, and emptied her tray. She walked out of the cafeteria and into a small, gray town near Pittsburgh. I wanted her to *be* Alice. I wanted her to smile as if she loved me. I wanted her to say, "Buck up, kiddo, everything's going to be all right." And what I'm trying to tell you now is this: I grew up in a split-level ranch-style house outside a town that could have been anywhere. I grew up in front of a television. I would have believed her.

[Hallway]

The story goes like this: my sister was born angry. She had colic as a newborn and cried for six weeks. After that, she just cried. We lived then with my maternal grandparents in North Carolina. My father was away on temporary duty in the air force and traveled the western part of the country, installing radar systems. Mama did not want to be alone in a bad neighborhood in Texas with two babies in diapers. She and Granny Ledbetter stayed up in shifts. Shelly wore them both out. Paw-paw could not stand to hear a baby cry. He was soft-hearted and nervous. He paced and smoked and sat and rocked on the porch. Shelly cried and cried. I was the only person in the house who slept much. I was fifteen months old, and had spent my life until then in small houses beneath the runway approaches of air force bases. Shelly had dark skin and black hair and eyes when she was born, but fair skin and blonde hair and blue eyes by the time Daddy came back from TDY. He did not recognize her. She cried when he picked her up. Everyone agreed that Shelly cried because she was mad, but they could not figure out what she was mad about. It is said that the only thing that would make her stop crying in the morning was the sound of my grandfather's footsteps in the hallway.

—◊◊◊—

Or this: my great-grandmother kicked my great-grandfather out of their bed after my grandfather was born. My great-grandfather, Bill Ledbetter, slept in the hallway, near the front door, beside the steps leading upstairs. The hallway was unheated, and in the winter he slept under a great pile of quilts. In the summer he slept with the front and back doors open and lay comfortably in the breeze that traveled between the doors late at night.

One evening, during the second world war, a Bible salesman stopped by the house. The house was close to no town, the road by it unpaved. Whole days went by without a car passing. The Bible salesman seemed particularly lost. He struggled with a heavy black suitcase. He was on foot and did not speak English. It was near sundown. He made gestures with his hands and tried out strange words over and over. He looked from one uncomprehending face to another. My family had never heard anyone speak a foreign language. They could not tell what language it was. With hand signals Bill Ledbetter offered the Bible salesman a bed for the night. This was in a different time. He showed the Bible salesman a room upstairs. He motioned for the Bible salesman to open the suitcase. Bill Ledbetter looked inside and nodded at the Bibles he saw there and took the lamp and went back downstairs.

That night the Bible salesman did not sleep. He paced the floor of his room, from one side to the other, all night long. Everyone downstairs listened. My mother was a little girl. She climbed in bed with my grandparents. My uncle Tom crawled in with my great-grandmother. (My Aunt Barbara wasn't born yet.) Everyone lay still in the dark and stared straight up while the Bible salesman walked the floor above their heads. Bill Ledbetter got out of his bed and very quietly took his shotgun down from the halltree. He placed it in the bed beside him. He covered it with the sheet and lay awake in the hallway and listened.

—m—

BILL LEDBETTER hired the carpenter Guilford Nanney to build the house for him in 1917, in the fork of a road, down the hill from Rock Springs Baptist Church. The site is on an upland farm, on the spine of a ridge ringed in the distance by mountains. The house is white, surrounded on three sides by a porch. The steep roof is covered with red tin, through which the upstairs dormer windows peer out. The hallway is forty-one feet long and just over six feet wide. It bisects the middle of the house. Its ceiling is nine feet, two inches high. Its walls and ceiling are unfinished heart pine tongue and groove, red and dark now with age. The walls are marked with hundreds of faint, yellow streaks where for years Paw-paw struck stick matches to light his cigarettes. The streaks are curved upwards at the ends, like fish hooks, where the match sparked and Paw-paw lifted it away from the wall. The floor is made of four-inch pine boards, which were covered with carpet in 1978.

If you stand at the front door and look down the hallway to the back of the house, you will see on your left the doors to the living room, dining room, and kitchen. On your right you will see two windows, the halltree, the stairway curving up, the doors to the canning closet beneath the stairs, and two bedrooms. My family knows the bedrooms as the front room and the back room. The doors, stair steps, banister, and railing are also unfinished pine. The doors have brass knobs; the railing is bright, and smooth enough to slide on. Three rooms are upstairs: the big room, the junk room, and Uncle

Tom's room. My grandmother is displeased by the junk room. Early in their marriages her children asked her if they could store a few things upstairs that they did not have room for in their small, rented houses, and then never came back to get them.

—⁓—

BEFORE SHE married Bill Ledbetter, my great-grandmother was Sallie Ursula Egerton. The Egertons, it is said, were granted a significant chunk of western North Carolina by an English king. Nobody remembers anymore exactly how much land, or even which king. It is doubtful that even the Egertons at the time ever fully realized the extent of their holdings. They were rich as only people in a new world can be rich. They owned everything they could see. They owned the mountains in the distance. But generations passed. The Egertons married local. There was no one else to marry. They gradually began to forget where they were from. They came to think of themselves as Carolinians, and then Americans, and then Confederates. They divided their land among themselves and among the mountain boys who married their daughters, and then divided it again. Over the course of two hundred years, North Carolina changed them from English aristocracy to country people with straight backs. Their dignity survived intact, but the family itself did not take a good hold. Their numbers did not improve over time, and their lot diminished. They began to die out.

—⁓—

While we lived with Granny and Paw-paw, Mama put my playpen in the hallway, in the spot where Bill Ledbetter's bed used to be, so I could see out the front door. Paw-paw's beagles occasionally stopped at the screen and looked in. This made me laugh. Mama and Granny were busy with Shelly, or napping for the next shift. They were not able to pay me much attention. I sat in the playpen, so the story goes, and looked at a *Reader's Digest*. I did not chew on it. I did not rip the pages out. Once I fell asleep with it covering my face. I would not touch a *Progressive Farmer* or look at a *Life*. Do not ask me why. Paw-paw drove an old, green Lincoln. Mama and Granny say that every afternoon I announced his impending arrival by making a noise like a car.

—⁓—

The last Egerton to live on the Egerton homeplace on Walnut Creek was my great-grandmother's uncle, Tom Egerton. People said that Tom Egerton wasn't right. He never married and lived alone in a dignified, bewildered squalor. His dogs and chickens wandered in and out of the house. Some people believed he had a fortune squirreled away; his father had been known as Squire, and the Egerton slaves were buried on the hill above the house. The way Tom Egerton lived made the people who believed in the fortune angry. They tried to cheat him out of money. It felt to them like a right, a settling up. Tom Egerton gave away what little money he had, and offered the people who came to cheat him sweet potatoes. He cooked the potatoes in the coals in his fireplace. His obliviousness and eccentricity embarrassed the few Egertons who were left. By the end of his life, Tom Egerton had to sleep in the crib to keep people from stealing his corn. After he died, people broke into his house and ripped down the wallboards and pried up the hearth stones. My great-grandmother inherited his farm. It became known as Bill Ledbetter's. My family refers to it as "down on the creek."

—⁓—

BY THE TIME the sun came up, everyone in the house was afraid of the Bible salesman. The pacing had not stopped all night long. Bill Ledbetter and my grandfather did not leave the house that morning to do their chores. Sallie Ledbetter and my grandmother herded my mother and Uncle Tom into the kitchen and ordered them to be quiet. When the Bible salesman came downstairs Bill Ledbetter offered him breakfast. Decorum would not permit him to do otherwise. My grandmother cooked eggs and grits and ham and biscuits as fast as she could. She cut up a cantaloupe but did not remove the rind.

Bill Ledbetter showed the Bible salesman a place at the dining-room table. The Bible salesman ate with his fingers. Granny brought the food in from the kitchen. He ate everything they heaped on his plate. He ate seconds and thirds. He ate all the biscuits in the basket and all the ham on the platter. He ate everything that was left on the table. My family was used to feeding field hands, men with large appetites who worked all day in the sun and maybe didn't have much food at home, but they had never seen anyone eat like the Bible salesman. He saved his cantaloupe slices for last. He ate the sweet meat, then he ate the rinds. Bill Ledbetter passed his cantaloupe rinds down the table. The Bible salesman ate them, too. When all the food was gone he stood and nodded and talked at them in strange words. He picked up his big suitcase and left the house and walked away up the ridge. My family watched him going up the road past the church until he was out of sight. They returned to the dining room and sat down around the table.

During the long night in his bed in the hallway, Bill Ledbetter had figured things out. The Bible salesman's suitcase had a false bottom. Beneath the false bottom the suitcase contained bombs and guns. The strange language he spoke was German. Bill Ledbetter was angry at himself for not figuring things out sooner. My family sat around the dining-room table until far in the morning; the cows went without milking, the chickens without scratch. They gazed at the plate the Bible salesman had eaten from as if it were a relic. It was as clean as if a dog had licked it. They looked gratefully at each other. They did not say so, but were glad they had lived through the night.

—៳៳—

BILL LEDBETTER married up. Sallie Egerton married well. Bill Ledbetter was a huge, strong man. In pictures his face is biblical and sharp, like Lincoln's. As a young man he watched the sun rise and set with the reins from his team of plow horses draped around his neck. The fields turned green and lush behind him. He started with nothing save prodigious strength and an unreasonable ambition, but was prosperous by the time he married Sallie Egerton. He opened a general store. He bought a second farm, black bottomland on the Broad River. When his wife inherited Tom Egerton's place, he made the days long enough to work three farms at once. He hired field hands to help him, many of them black men named Egerton. Lazy men could not work for Bill Ledbetter. He ran them off if they didn't quit first. When he hoed or picked cotton, he lapped everyone else in the field. He had water hauled to the hands in the rows so they would not waste time walking to the bucket.

One year he planted the largest bottom on the old Egerton

farm in head lettuce. People rode to the bottom from miles around to look at it. Few farmers then even grew lettuce in their gardens. Truck farming was unheard of. Sweet potatoes and cotton and tobacco were the only cash crops people thought to plant. Visitors to the bottom looked at the carefully hoed grid of lettuce hills stretching away toward the creek and snickered. They said Bill Ledbetter wouldn't be able to pay his help. But when the lettuce was ripe, Bill Ledbetter crated it up, stacked the crates into a tall, teetering load on the bed of his truck, and hauled it over the mountains to the farmers' market in Knoxville. He sold it for a dollar a head. People began to consider Bill Ledbetter's opinions carefully. Farmers planted head lettuce when he planted head lettuce and cucumbers when he planted cucumbers. He was elected to the school board. He taught himself to read music and with a tuning fork led the singing at Rock Springs Baptist Church. He traveled to Raleigh and told state legislators what was on his mind. In 1917, as he came into his own, he hired Guilford Nanney to build him a house.

—⟋⟋⟋—

MY COUSINS and I loved running up and down the hallway, but Paw-paw and Granny did not like for us to run inside the house. He was afraid we would fall and get hurt; she was afraid one of Paw-paw's guns would fall to the floor and discharge and kill us. Paw-paw kept shotguns and rifles hanging from the hat hooks on the halltree, and from the hat hooks on the wall. All of his guns stayed loaded. Paw-paw said there was no reason to keep a gun in the house if it wasn't loaded. Granny said there was no reason to keep a gun in the house if it was. This was one of the few points on which I ever heard them disagree.

Running up and down the hallway was one of the few ways we even considered disobeying Paw-paw and Granny. They were loathe to spank us and rarely had to. We found the thought that one of them might be angry at us deterrent enough. But the hallway was our temptation, a fine line along the edge of their good graces. It was long enough to race in full speed. It demanded we run. Our feet pounding on the wooden floor thundered inside the tall, enclosed space. We became a herd, a posse. The brass doorknobs rattled as we passed. We made more noise than we absolutely had to. We made an altogether satisfactory racket.

Even under direct orders, a sideways look as we came into the front door was enough to propel the whole lot of us down the hallway. What happened then was always the same. Paw-paw rapped his knuckles against the living-room wall and said, "I'm gonna jerk a knot in somebody's tail," but by then we were pulling up at the opposite end of the house, where we met Granny coming out of the kitchen.

She said, "You jaybirds stop all that running before one of those guns falls."

———

Guilford Nanney traveled the countryside building the tall houses he saw in his head. He was not a carpenter to whom you could present a plan drawn by someone else. You told him how many rooms you wanted, and he built you a house. That was the transaction. He would not suffer interference and meddling. The inordinate length of the hallway, the extravagant line and steep pitch of the roof were his idea alone. He lived in a small shack on the property, and started work mornings as soon as he could see. He sawed all of the framing for Bill Ledbetter's house and piled it in the front yard before he ever drove a nail. He did not use a blueprint, but when he put the house together, all the pieces fit. There were no studs or rafters or joists left over. He did not find this remarkable. The roof, seen from any angle, comprises a series of triangles, offset so that your eye is drawn upward as it is when you look at mountains and find yourself seeking the tallest peak. From the front door, the back door at the other end of the house seems as far away as the altar of a cathedral. The landing at the top of the stairs is cantilevered, and floats out over the hallway without betraying the intricacy of the structure that supports it, or the complexity of thought behind it.

———〰———

MY COUSINS and sister ran barefoot up and down the hallway in the summer, and someone always pulled up lame and
crying, with a long, jagged splinter impaled in the heel or toe.
Granny rounded up the injured cousin and sat him or her down
in a straight chair in the kitchen. She dug at the splinter with
a needle sterilized in alcohol. The cousin screamed and flailed;
Granny threatened and scolded and cajoled. She swore that in
just a minute she was going to pop somebody if the racket
didn't stop; she said she would get a switch after the whole lot
of us if we didn't get out of her light so she could see.

When the splinter came loose she presented it to the sob-
bing cousin for inspection. She applied red Mercurochrome,
which didn't burn, or orange Methylate, which did, to the
wound. We all sucked in our breath and watched the cousin's
face when it was Methylate. The cousin limped down the
hallway with the needle to show the splinter to Paw-paw.
The rest of us followed along behind, grumbling by then at
the cousin's hysteria. Paw-paw took the cousin up into his lap
and patted him or her on the leg and pretended not to be able
to see the splinter, it was so small. He looked carefully at the
red or orange stain on the bottom of the cousin's foot and
said that he thought it was going to be all right. The rest of
us gathered around Paw-paw's chair and leaned toward him.
He smelled like aftershave and Vitalis. Each of us secretly

wished we had been fortunate enough to have been injured so grievously.

—✺—

IT IS SAID that as Bill Ledbetter watched the tall, skeletal peaks of his new roof rising, he was sickened by the amount of lumber Guilford Nanney used. Bill Ledbetter was not by nature an extravagant man. He wanted a big house, but could not sanction waste. While it is unknown whether he said anything to Guilford Nanney about what he considered gratuitous use of material, it is known that Guilford Nanney left the job suddenly while there was still trim work to be done around the doors and windows upstairs. He took a job building the first set of steps to the top of Chimney Rock, a mountain visible from Bill Ledbetter's front yard. Rich men were making the mountain into a park. No one knows if Bill Ledbetter complained about Guilford Nanney's desertion. He simply finished the house himself. While Bill Ledbetter's carpentry work is level and adequate and square, it is not hard to spot. The only hammer marks in the whole house belong to Bill Ledbetter. It is easy to tell at the top of the stairs where one man left a job, and another man took it up.

—✺—

SALLIE LEDBETTER was never a robust woman and did not bear children easily. The first child she had with Bill Ledbetter was a girl, Clydie Belle. Clydie was frail from the time of her birth and did not live to see a healthy day. She died of colitis when she was seven months old. Their second child, a son, was born prematurely and lived only an hour. They did not name him. My grandfather, William Dan, was their third and last child. As a baby he was small and sickly and Sallie Ledbetter feared for his health. She kept him in her bed to keep him warm. She was afraid Bill Ledbetter would turn over on the baby in his sleep and banished him to another bed.

When Bill Ledbetter moved his family into the new house Guilford Nanney built, he put his bed in the hallway and slept there for the next thirty years. My grandfather slept in the front room, in the bed with his mother, until he was a tall and gangly boy. When Bill Ledbetter finally made Paw-paw move to another room, Sallie Ledbetter did not ask him to return to her bed, or perhaps by then he did not want to go. My family is unsure how this part of the story goes. Bill Ledbetter did not sleep again in the same room with his wife until 1947, when he was an old man sick with lung cancer. He had his bed moved to the front room from the hallway because in his illness he could no longer keep warm.

—⁓—

My story goes like this: I jerked the front screen door open and ran as hard as I could. The house was Fenway Park in Boston, the hallway the first-base path. The door swinging shut behind me was a throw whizzing in from first. If I hit the back door before the front door slammed, I was safe. If the front door slammed first, I was out. I hit the back screen running and crossed the porch in a step and jumped off into the yard and kept going. I went for extra bases. The game then became problematic, a matter of judgment and honesty. The spring on the back door was pulling it closed. The clothesline pole was too close, too easy to reach in time, to be an acceptable base; the woodshed was too far away. There was no quantitative way to make the call of safe or out. I had to decide when the door slammed where I was on the field. Sometimes I slowed up with a single, disappointed skip and slapped my hands on my thighs and turned toward the dugout. I was out. Sometimes I clapped my hands once and reached out to accept the congratulatory handshake of an imaginary teammate. *Earley scores! He has good speed! He's having a heck of a year!* In my mind's eye, I was always on television. I interviewed myself in the woodshed, where no one could see me from the house. I took off my cap and wiped my brow with the back of my arm. I spoke into a piece of kindling. I said, *"Thanks. I felt good today. I'm just glad I could help the team."*

—⟋⟍—

A CORNER cupboard from the Egerton homeplace used to sit in the dining room. It was built by Egerton slaves out of wide oak boards. It was big and dark and solid as a vault. When I was a little kid I had to stand on a chair to see what was inside it. Paw-paw stored his tools on the top three shelves. Behind the wide doors he kept dark, heavy wrenches and hammers and screwdrivers and files, and old coffee cans filled with nuts and bolts and screws and the occasional, odd shotgun shell. There were leftover balls of baling twine, and twisted leather gloves fragrant with grease, and inscrutable pieces of machinery, parts of tractors and balers and combines and trucks; there were chains and spare tines from cultivators and planters and plows. Granny kept tablecloths and towels and napkins and washcloths on the bottom two shelves. The cupboard smelled like washing powder and clean cotton stiffened by the sun—like rust and leather and creosote. It smelled simultaneously like a warm barn and fresh sheets.

Paw-paw showed the cupboard once to an antiques dealer. The man wanted immediately to buy it. He tried to buy it for years. Paw-paw did not sell it until 1978, after he was sick, when the house had begun to seem big and cold. The antiques dealer gave five hundred dollars for the cupboard. Paw-paw and Granny used the money to carpet the hallway. Granny says today that she does not wish the cupboard back, even though it would be worth thousands of dollars. She says the only furniture she's ever known was dark and ponderous and ugly to look at. Much of it came from the Egertons' and was old already when she married Dan Ledbetter in 1933 and moved into the house. She does not understand the modern Southern passion for antiques. She would not walk to the mailbox for a truckload. She has wanted her whole life to get rid of old things and replace them with new. She especially does not miss sweeping the hallway. Forty-five years was long enough. She memorized the grain in the flooring. She wore out more brooms than she cares to remember. She still considers the cupboard for the carpet a good trade.

—ᴍ—

And this: Granny and Paw-paw slept in the front room. Paw-paw kept a loaded .38 revolver in a cigar box in the nightstand by the bed. On Sundays after church I used to sneak down the hallway and into their room to look at it. It was a black, antique Smith & Wesson. I was strictly forbidden to touch it. One Sunday I pulled the hammer back and cocked it. At that moment I felt the gun become a living thing in my hand. It felt dangerous as a coiled snake. I was afraid to breathe. I was nine or ten years old. I didn't know what to do. I couldn't call for help because I would get into trouble; I couldn't put it back into the cigar box because it was cocked.

I was afraid to uncock the gun because it might fire. I had seen people uncock guns on television hundreds of time. They held the hammer back with a thumb and pulled the trigger, but they were Marshall Dillon and Mannix and McGarrett and Gil Favor. If the hammer slipped from beneath my thumb the gun would go off. It would kill me or shoot through one of the walls. I became conscious of where my family was in the house. Mama and Granny were in the kitchen cooking dinner. Daddy was in the living room reading and Paw-paw was sitting on the front porch with his feet on the railing. I didn't know where Shelly was. There seemed to be no safe place to point the gun. I was sure I was going to kill someone, and the fear I felt turned also into a kind of sadness, and anticipation of loss. I moaned out loud, although I did not want or mean to. I prayed for God to help me. I gasped and closed my eyes and pulled the trigger. The gun did not fire. The hammer came loose between my thumbs and I held it poised for a moment above the firing pin. Then I lowered it slowly into place. The gun returned to sleep in my hand. I placed it back in the cigar box. I put the cigar box back in the nightstand. I wiped my hands on my pants and backed into the hallway. I ran down the hallway hard as I could and through the back door and across the porch and jumped off into the yard. I was almost to the woodshed before the back door slammed.

—⚬—

IT IS A credit to my grandmother that to this day she will not speak ill of Sallie Ledbetter. Granny's maiden name was Clara Mae Womack. She grew up on a small farm where Walnut Creek empties into the Green River, several miles below Tom Egerton's place. She married Dan Ledbetter in 1933, when she was nineteen years old. He was twenty-eight. She did not kiss him until they were engaged, and then she put a chair between them so he couldn't get his arms around her. They had planned to live in the small house the Ledbetters had lived in before the big house was built, but Sallie Ledbetter forbade her son to move out. Later she had the older house torn down.

While the big house with the red roof was known as Bill Ledbetter's place, it was Sallie Ledbetter who decreed what was what inside it. When Clara Mae Ledbetter moved in, Sallie Ledbetter stopped cooking altogether. Granny cooked breakfast before dawn, a big dinner for the field hands at noon, and supper for the family in the evening. She did most of the cleaning and washing. Her life was not easy. If she and Paw-paw went upstairs together during the day, Sallie Ledbetter called her daughter-in-law back downstairs because it did not look proper. She scolded the two of them if they went for a walk alone.

When my uncle Tom was born, Sallie Ledbetter insisted the

baby sleep with her. The room Paw-paw and Granny slept in did not have a stove, and Sallie Ledbetter said the baby would get sick in the cold. She did not express the same concern later for my mother and my aunt Barbara, who slept in unheated rooms from the time they were born until they married and moved away. Uncle Tom slept with Sallie Ledbetter until he was a tall and gangly boy. She would not let him eat watermelon because she thought watermelon had given Clydie the colitis that killed her. Granny could not put her foot down because it was not her house, and Paw-paw would not stand up to his mother. Bill Ledbetter had no interest in the affairs of women. Inside the house Sallie Ledbetter's every wish hardened into stone as soon as she uttered it. Granny had nowhere to turn. She could not run the house the way she saw fit until Sallie Egerton Ledbetter died in 1953. Sallie Ledbetter also died of lung cancer, although neither she nor Bill Ledbetter ever smoked.

—⁂—

I CHASED my cousin Janet up the front steps. She squealed and opened the front door and ran into the house. We started down the hallway at a dead run. The screen door slammed behind us. A double-barreled twenty-gauge shotgun slipped from the top row of hat hooks on the halltree and fell and clattered onto the floor. Janet and I stopped in our tracks. We tiptoed back down the hallway and stared at the shotgun. It hadn't fired.

Paw-paw ran from the living room. Granny came down the hallway at a gallop from the kitchen. The falling gun had split the halltree seat half in two. Janet and I were terrified. We said that we hadn't done it, that we were just running down the hallway and the gun fell. Paw-paw's face flushed red. He began to shake. His fists were clenched at his sides. We could tell he didn't know what to do next. Janet and I held our breath. We had never seen him that angry.

"Damn," Paw-paw said.

"Dan!" Granny said. Paw-paw didn't believe in cursing.

"Damn, damn, damn, damn, damn," Paw-paw said. He seemed to like it, though, once he got started. He unbuckled his belt. He had never whipped any of us before. Granny did all the spanking, and she popped us so lightly that sometimes it was hard not to laugh. Paw-paw jerked his belt out through the loops. Janet and I began to cry. Paw-paw was tall as a giant. "How many times have I told you not to run in this house?" he said.

"Please don't whip us, Paw-paw," we said.

"Dan Ledbetter," Granny said, "you're not going to whip anybody. You're lucky that gun didn't go off. I've told you and told you not to keep those guns loaded."

Paw-paw and Granny stared at each other and went out the

front door and down the steps and around the side of the house. Janet and I tiptoed into the living room and peeked out the window. We could see them arguing through the gap between the two heating oil tanks at the side of the house, but the window was closed and we couldn't hear what they said. We had never seen them argue before and it scared us to watch. Paw-paw still held his belt in his hand. Janet said later she thought they were going to get a divorce.

Paw-paw pointed at the house and said something angry to Granny. We could tell he was talking about us. Granny pointed at the house and said something angry back. She was talking about him. Paw-paw spun away from her and walked away. We ran to the window on the other side of the room to see where he went. He walked quickly across the front yard and got in his car and drove away. Granny came back inside and ordered me into the back room and Janet into the front room. She told us that if she heard one sound out of either of us she would get a switch after us, and we could tell she meant what she said. I don't know about Janet, but I cried into the pillow on the bed in the back room. I was sure Paw-paw hated me.

—⁊⁊—

WHILE DAN Ledbetter grew to be as tall as Bill Ledbetter, he did not inherit his father's strength or stamina. He was 6'4", but so skinny that he seemed to have been constructed from spare parts. In photographs his legs seem much too long and delicate, the rest of his body ill-supported, dangerously high above the ground. Only near the end of his life, when he grew a small, incongruous potbelly, did he ever weigh more than one hundred and fifty pounds. He wore only long-sleeved shirts, whose cuffs he kept tightly buttoned at the wrist. And if he suffered in physical comparison with Bill Ledbetter, Paw-paw fared no better in comparison of accomplishment. Even on a tractor, he could never do in a day the work his father did in the same amount of time with a team of horses. The sun never stood still above the fields in which he worked.

Bill Ledbetter's strength was an act of nature: random and unique, indifferent and cruel as a storm. He lived in solitude inside his great body. He did not understand weakness because he had never known it; he was oblivious as a tree to the straining of the lesser bodies around him. When he stood at the front of the Rock Springs Baptist Church on Sunday mornings and tapped his tuning fork on the communion table and held it to his ear, it seemed to him proper that only he could hear the note. For that reason he prevented the church from buying a piano until long after it would have otherwise done so.

Sunday afternoons Bill Ledbetter sat in the shade on the corner of the porch and with the tuning fork and sang his way through one of the Baptist hymnals he ordered from all over the country. The fields bloomed all around him while he sang. He offered the hymns as thanks to God. His family gathered around him and listened, but only listened; he did not ask them to join him. He was a man of faith, but his understanding of God revolved only around the work he could do himself between dawn and dark, six days a week, and the countable ways that work was rewarded. It did not occur to him that other men might strike their own deals with God in different currencies. He never thought to teach his only son the things he had learned.

That people looked to Dan Ledbetter to match his father in word and deed, when he was incapable of doing so, was perhaps my grandfather's heaviest burden. While Bill Ledbetter delighted in firing both barrels of his massive 10-gauge shotgun at once, Paw-paw found shooting the gun one barrel at a time as unpleasant as any other ordinary man. The one time Paw-paw fired both barrels simultaneously, the recoil turned him around in his tracks. He never planted a cash crop for which there was a demand a year before there was a supply. He never considered his opinions worthy of a journey to Raleigh. He never bought land or led the singing in church. He spent his life presiding over the slow dissipation of Bill Ledbetter's immaculate farms. Through no fault of his own he became the measuring stick people used to construct Bill Ledbetter's legend. That stick was in turn used to measure him.

—⁓—

After a while Paw-paw blew the horn in the front yard. Janet and I opened the doors and looked tentatively out into the hallway. Every day Paw-paw rode down on the creek to feed the cows. It was a favorite expedition among the cousins. Granny came out of the kitchen with Paw-paw's cap and a plastic margarine dish filled with food scraps from dinner. Paw-paw always took food scraps for the cats who lived in the barn. The cats rubbed against his legs, but ran away when we tried to touch them. Granny motioned for us to follow her and walked down the hallway and held the screen door open. She handed me the scraps for the cats and Paw-paw's cap. Paw-paw didn't like to go anywhere without his cap. He had left the house without it earlier. "Go on out there," Granny said. "He's not mad at you."

Janet and I went slowly down the front steps and walked across the yard toward the car. The motor was running. Paw-paw watched us through the windshield. We walked up close to the car and stopped. I couldn't tell if he was mad or not. I was afraid to say anything. I handed him his cap through the window. He said, "You knotheads going with me?"

We ran around the car and opened the door and climbed

in. Janet slid up close beside Paw-paw. I rolled down the window. On the way to the creek Paw-paw stopped at Ed Bailey's store and bought each of us a Mountain Dew and a pack of M&M's. He did not mention the halltree, then or ever. He had a carpenter glue the two halves of the seat back together. If you examine the seat today, you cannot tell it was ever broken.

—⁓—

BILL LEDBETTER made no provision for his family after his passing, other than leaving them the land he had accumulated over the years. He did not believe in insurance. When his general store burned down years before, he had not been able to replace it. He died in 1947 after a long stay at Baptist Hospital in Winston-Salem, leaving behind a sheaf of bills thick enough to be the story of his life. My family found itself land rich, but cash poor. Paw-paw had to sell the farm on the river to pay the medical bills. That first spring, he had to hire someone to lay out the corn rows in the remaining Ledbetter bottoms because he didn't know how. He was forty-two years old and had farmed his entire life, but his father had never trusted him with anything important. Bill Ledbetter had reserved for himself the labors that required thought or skill. The fields Paw-paw planted in sweet potatoes that year came up in Johnson grass and did not make a crop.

—⁓—

For years I tried to jump high enough to touch the ceiling in the hallway. In the slow movement of time as it is measured by children, I had been trying to touch the ceiling forever. I never came close until the Sunday my middle finger brushed the wood. I was fourteen years old and could not believe I had finally done it. I jumped again to verify what had happened, and again my middle finger brushed the dark pine. I had crossed some threshold I couldn't name, but felt a profound, if equally nameless, pleasure at finding myself on the other side. One Sunday I couldn't jump high enough to touch a ceiling nine feet, two inches above the floor, but the next Sunday I could. This simple fact came to stand during my adolescence as a constant, quantifiable measurement of *something*. I checked it every Sunday the way a meteorologist might check gauges. That I could always touch the ceiling when I jumped provided a small, welcome comfort, a slight marking of joy.

Soon I could touch the ceiling with increasingly larger portions of my hand: two fingers, then three fingers, then four. By the time Shelly died in December 1979 I could jump high enough to place both palms flat against the ceiling. I checked this measurement immediately after her funeral, still wearing my suit and dress shoes. Paw-paw died the following June, shortly before my nineteenth birthday, of heart disease and emphysema. If my family thought I was being disrespectful by jumping in the hallway after his funeral, while the house was still full of visitors, I don't remember them telling me so.

After Shelly died I continued jumping in the hallway, but came to view the fact that I could still slap my hands on the ceiling as verification of nothing so much as God's unfairness. I wanted to know why Shelly had died and I had lived; I became so adamant in the face of the unanswerable that my life unraveled around the question. Shelly's lifelong anger not only filled me with regret at the times I had deserved to be its object, but with certainty that it had been a premonition she had been unable to voice. I hadn't understood what she was trying to say until it was too late to make amends. Although we no doubt loved each other, we never really got along. It seemed to me then, and—in the secret part of my heart where I hold unreasonable truths—seems to me still, that Shelly came into this world knowing she would not be here long. She spent her short life in a howl of protest untranslatable by the people she loved most.

I also came to believe that I was somehow a beneficiary of Shelly's death, that an account had been settled in my favor. I began to think I was invincible. I thought I would live forever. My jumping took on a desperate, daredevil quality. In the woods behind Granny's house I vaulted over the chest-high barbed-wire fence that separated her property from her neighbor's. I took running starts and leaped over picnic tables and shrubs, and once over a parked MG Midget. I stood flat-footed and jumped over chairs, trash cans, lengthwise over coffee tables, up four, five, six steps of my dormitory stairwell. What I did not take into account when jumping was the accumulated violence of landing. I jumped as if my immortality had been bought and paid for, without realizing that each time my feet hit the ground I paid a corresponding physical price. Eventually, my knees and feet began to give out. By the time I was twenty-five, I was hesitant to jump over the net on a tennis court, a leap I would have taken without thinking a few years before. I was afraid of how much it would hurt when I landed.

As I write this, I no longer jump particularly well. On a good day I can touch the hallway ceiling with my three longest fingers. Although I didn't realize it at the time, the thing I began measuring with that first jump was the inevitable arc of my own mortality. The day is approaching when I won't be able to touch the ceiling at all. And while I realize the vanity and uselessness and ingratitude inherent in any evaluation of self-worth based solely on accomplishment of the body, it is still a day I dread. I am sensitive to the power of metaphor to the point of superstition. It was metaphor that frightened Bill Ledbetter the first morning the cancer sprouting in his lungs prevented him from going to the fields and doing a day's work. Metaphor was the stranger outside in the dark from whom my grandfather sought to protect himself and his family with the shotguns and rifles that lined the hallway, and it was metaphor that rode as a friend in his left breast pocket until it finally killed him. It was metaphor that left sulfurous tracks on the walls of the hallway you can still see today. The last five years of his life Paw-paw had to sleep sitting up in order to catch his breath. While I cannot recall the sound of his voice, I can still hear him cough. It was metaphor that kept us all awake and listening during those nights. We were afraid with each cough that Paw-paw was going to die, until eventually he did. The metaphors of his life hardened into facts. That I remember almost nothing of what my sister said to me is a fact. That Granny is eighty-six years old is a fact. I wish that with these words I could turn the hallway into perfect metaphor, an incantation that would restore everyone who ever walked its length to the person they wanted most in their best heart to be, but the fact is that the hallway is simply a space forty-one feet long, nine feet, two inches high, and just over six feet wide, through which my family has traveled for eighty-four years. Of all the facts we have gathered and stored in the hallway, this one troubles me most: stories in real life rarely end the way we want them to. They simply end.

[Deer Season, 1974]

The winter I was thirteen years old, I wasn't allowed in the woods with a gun until my father got home from work at four-thirty—which left me less than an hour of shooting time before dark. That I managed to kill twelve squirrels, two rabbits, and a quail under such adverse conditions seemed to me then a mark of considerable prowess, a measure of worth greater than anything I had mustered previously. I hadn't learned yet that the things I would spend the rest of my life hunting for didn't live in the woods, nor had the sheer excitement of slipping through the trees with a loaded gun been surpassed by the instantaneous regret I felt whenever I watched an animal thump to the ground dead, or, wounded, try to crawl away.

I never headed for home until after dark, during the small period of grace between dusk and the time I knew I would get into trouble. I trotted through the trees in what I hoped was Indian style, amazed by how bright the woods seemed in the starlight. I imagined that had anyone been watching me, my eyes would have glowed like a cat's. When I jogged into the open, the lights of our house across the pasture glared so brightly it seemed impossible that the light itself was not accompanied by sound. Only when I crept into the yard, careful to stay out of the light, could I hear my sister's stereo, the news on television, my mother running water in the kitchen. Before I stepped out of the shadows, I broke open my shotgun and removed the single shell from the chamber. I had promised my parents at the start of hunting season that I would unload the gun the moment it became too dark to shoot, but I never did. Unloaded, my shotgun never seemed to me more than simply a heavy thing to carry home. I dropped the shell into my pocket. I didn't want to go inside; that year, being alone in the woods seemed preferable to being anywhere else. Our dog barked from the back steps. I called his name, crossed the carport, and clumped into the kitchen. Some nights I held up something dead for whoever was in the kitchen to see; some nights I didn't. That was the winter my father finally agreed to take me deer hunting.

The morning of Opening Day he woke me by calling my

name the single time he said he would. I pulled on a pair of long underwear, two pairs of jeans, and four or five pairs of socks. I shoved my feet into the embarrassing pair of two-toned, slick-bottomed, zip-up boots my mother had bought at Pic N' Pay. Before I had been awake ten minutes, we were clattering in my father's Volkswagen toward the steep, laureled ridges of Green River Cove, the next county over, the magical country where deer lived. Long before daylight I was sitting on a rough board nailed between two limbs of a pine tree, staring into the blackness of a ravine through which a small creek gurgled toward Lake Adger. My father left me and went off to his own deer stand. Within ten minutes I wanted to go home. I had never been so cold in my life. Then it started to sleet. By the time the sky began to lighten, my feet hurt terribly. Inside my gloves, the tips of my fingers began to sting. And I had to go to the bathroom. My father had told me not to climb down from the tree until he came back. But I knew that if I didn't climb down, I would mess my pants long before he came after me. I also felt that I would die from the cold if I didn't move. So I climbed down.

The deer came up out of the ravine while my pants were down around my ankles. In the thin light I couldn't tell if the black shape was a buck or a doe, only that it was a deer. I squinted and tried to make out horns. Without moving my head I glanced at my shotgun leaning against the tree beside me. I wondered if the deer could see my butt. When I reached for the gun, the deer leaped and vanished noisily down the side of the ravine. It ran for a long time. I sat and listened until the sound of the deer running melted away into the sound of the sleet hissing on the leaves. I pulled up my pants, picked up my gun, and climbed back into the tree. I didn't stay long. My teeth chattered so hard that they began to ache. I knew that my father would be disappointed in me, but I couldn't take the cold any longer.

When I got to the car, I unloaded my shotgun, then climbed in and turned on the radio. I curled up on the backseat and pulled my father's old overcoat over my head. Soon I was warm and comfortable. I lay with my eyes open in the darkness underneath the coat. The sleet scratched at the roof and ticked against the windows, but it couldn't get at me. I remember clearly that "Blue Eyes Crying in the Rain" and "Kung Fu Fighting" played on the radio. As I listened to the music, I realized that I could make out the sound of each instrument playing individually, that if I chose I could listen to a single instrument to the exclusion of everything else around it. I felt as if I had discovered something extraordinary, that I understood how music worked in a way no one had before. Even "Kung Fu Fighting" seemed profound. I don't remember ever feeling happier. I began to imagine, even wish, that my father would never come back, that the sleet wouldn't stop, that the radio would continue to play, that I could lie forever in the warm and the dark and the music and never have to leave again.

After a while I heard my father jacking the shells from his deer rifle onto the ground. When he got into the car he didn't say anything. He turned off the radio and cranked the Volkswagen and drove down the old logging road toward Lake Adger and the highway. I tried to keep track of where we were by the direction the car traveled through the curves, but I was soon lost. We could have been going anywhere. After we had driven for some time, he said, "Boy, don't you know better than to shit under your tree?" That was all he had to say. I was instantly filled with shame. Of course I knew better. Deer have almost supernatural senses of smell. I knew that. What kind of hunter was I? I was stupid, stupid, stupid, that's what I was. I suddenly understood, with the clarity of a slap, that no matter how many squirrels I killed that winter—that even if I managed to kill a deer—I would be no closer to escaping childhood than I would have been if I had never walked into the woods with a gun. I was a kid, and would be a kid for longer than I had the heart to think about. I decided not to pull the coat from over my head, maybe never. I didn't tell my father about the deer I had scared away, and I never asked him to take me deer hunting again. I understand now that he was speaking only of deer hunting, and that I, simply because I

was thirteen years old, applied his hard question, by exten-
sion, to the rest of my life. I don't remember arriving home or
getting out of the car. I don't remember going to bed that
night, or getting up, or going to school. All I can say for sure,
all these years later, is that I must have done all those things.
But my memory of that morning ends in the car, somewhere
between Lake Adger and home. For all I can tell by remem-
bering, we are still on the road somewhere, my father—
who would be, miraculously, the same age I am now—and
behind him, hiding under an overcoat, the boy who shit under his tree.

[Shooting the Cat]

L *et me begin by saying this: all of us were fond of the cat. To a person we agreed that it was satisfactory, even remarkable, in all categories. The character or qualifications of the cat in no way influenced our decision to shoot it. We are not cruel people.*

—⁊⁊⁊—

WE DECIDED to shoot the cat on the third Sunday in May, the day our home church in North Carolina celebrates Memorial Day. My family was sitting together on the front porch of my grandmother's house. We had been to church. We had decorated the graves of our ancestors and relatives with potted plants and tall vases of mums and lilies. We had eaten lunch off of paper plates, beneath the oak trees behind the fellowship hall. We had changed out of our Sunday clothes. Some of us were drinking iced tea. The men sat with their feet up on the banisters. Somebody said, "Granny, where's your cat?"

The cat had come to Granny's house in the usual way: it showed up on the back steps freshly weaned and mewed solicitiously, as if seeking work. When you come over the top of the hill, the tall white house, with the road splitting around it, and mountains rising straight up on three sides in the near distance behind it, looks like a destination, even if it isn't the place for which you started out. It must resemble the picture of the idyllic farmhouse Americans carry in their collective subconscious like a snapshot, the one in which dwells the kindly farmer, part Grant Wood painting, part Disney dwarf, happy to adopt whatever unwanted pet someone may choose to abandon by the side of the road, because Granny, who has never really wanted a cat, has always had a cat on the place.

This particular cat was a ham, a prankster, a glutton for attention; that it was not underfoot was a puzzlement. It liked nothing better than stalking and leaping onto the feet of Granny's unsuspecting guests.

I said, "Kitty, kitty, kitty."

"Don't *call* it," Aunt Barbara said.

My father said, "That cat will aggravate you to death."

"The cat's sick," said Granny. "It hasn't eaten anything except a little milk in days. I wish somebody would get the gun and shoot it."

My cousin Marsha and I found the cat in the backyard. Its hip bones jutted sharply from its flanks; each of its vertebrae was distinct. I saw the hole in its neck when I picked it up. The fur around the hole was slick and wet. Inside the hole I briefly glimpsed the translucent white of exposed cartilage, and beyond the cartilage a secret, gaping blackness. I remember the moment as accompanied by a deafening noise, but, in reality, there was no sound at all, save that of the cat purring wetly in my arms. "Oh my God," Marsha said. "We've got to get it to a vet."

I strode up onto Granny's porch filled dangerously with mission. "A dog or something got hold of the cat," I announced. "It's got a big hole in its neck. We're going to take it to the vet."

I went into the house to use the phone. Granny followed me inside. "Who are you calling?" she said.

"I'm calling the vet," I said. The father of my best friend from high school was a veterinarian. I considered it an affirmative omen that after so many years I could remember their telephone number.

Granny told me to put down the phone. She said she wouldn't pay for taking a cat to the vet. I told her I would pay for it. The veterinarian's wife answered the phone. The vet was out. She would have him call me as soon as he got home.

"I think it's a waste of money," Granny said.

"I don't care what you think," I said. I had never spoken to Granny like that before. I left the house.

My cousin Greg came out to the backyard. Greg is Marsha's brother. "Nobody's taking the cat to the vet if Granny doesn't want it to go," he said.

I said, "I don't care what Granny wants."

"This is Granny's house, and that's her cat," Greg said. "We're going to do what she wants us to do. How would it make her feel if we told her she can't make her own decisions anymore?"

"I hadn't thought about it that way," I said.

Greg is by several years my youngest cousin, but he is often wise. The shape of the best thing to do began to change inside my head into something very different. He looked closely at the hole in the cat's neck. "It's got maggots in it," he said. "The vet probably couldn't save it anyway."

"Well," I said. "I guess that about does it."

I went into the house through the back door and called the vet's wife. I told her I wouldn't be bringing the cat. I went down the hall into the back room to get the pistol out of the cigar box in the nightstand.

Marsha appeared in the doorway. "What are you doing?" she said.

I didn't say anything. I took the pistol out of the box and stuck it into the pocket of my shorts.

"I can't believe you're doing this," Marsha said. She is a nurse, by profession and temperament. Caring for the sick is for Marsha an act of profoundest reflex. She doesn't have an uncompassionate bone in her body.

"It's got maggots in it, Marsha," I said. "The vet probably couldn't save it, anyway."

"You don't know that," Marsha said. "You don't go out and shoot something just because something that's bigger than it is got hold of it."

Greg and I walked up the old road that led through the pasture to the barn. Greg carried a shovel over his shoulder. I carried the cat. The pistol lay curled in my pocket. We passed the dog lot, the pig lot, the three apple trees between the pig lot and the barn, all of them overrun by poison oak vines. In recent years the poison oak had covered even the barn. Granny's place hasn't been a farm in a long time. Greg and I walked in the narrow path left in the center of the road. The open loft door of the barn gaped blackly out of the lush, green vines. I said, "Poison oak's taking over the place."

"Yep," Greg said. "We ought to come up here and spray it sometime."

We walked past the barn to the place where the road

disappeared into the spring woods. I said, "I guess this spot is as good as any."

"I guess so," said Greg.

I placed the cat on the ground, facing away from me. I drew the ancient .38 out of my pocket. Our grandfather had traded another gun for it years and years ago. I sighted down the barrel at the cat's head. I imagined the head changing shape in an instant to accommodate the bullet, the cat jerking once, dying. I pulled the trigger.

When the gun went off, the cat did an exaggerated double-take, one that might have been funny in different circumstances, say an old Tom and Jerry cartoon. It swiveled around and for an instant stared up at me. Then it leaped up and ran into the poison oak. I still pointed the pistol at a now-vacant spot on the ground.

"I think you missed it," Greg said.

—⟋⟍—

I SLIPPED into the back room to put the pistol back in the cigar box. Marsha was sitting on the bed. "Did you kill it?" she asked.

"No," I said. "I missed it."

"I called the sheriff's department," she said. "I could have you arrested. Cruelty to animals. All I have to do is call them back and agree to sign a warrant."

I was determined to kill the cat. I rummaged around upstairs until I found the only shotgun left in Granny's house. It was the Uncle Roland gun, a single-shot 12-gauge with an inordinately long barrel, famous in our family for going off unexpectedly. Only my grandmother's Uncle Roland had been brave enough to shoot it. Downstairs, I found a handful of discolored shells in an old box in the halltree and shoved them into my pocket. I walked out onto the front porch. Granny looked at the Uncle Roland gun and then up at me. "Where are you going with that thing?" she said.

"I missed the cat," I said.

"How far away were you?" my father asked.

"About two feet," I said.

"Well," Granny said.

"It's an old pistol, son," my father said. "You'd be lucky if you could hit the ground with it."

"Marsha's going to have me arrested."

"What for?" asked Aunt Barbara.

"Cruelty to animals."

"Not so far," said Aunt Katherine.

I walked back out to the barn. Greg eyed the Uncle Roland gun and moved a few steps away. We walked up and down the road calling "kitty, kitty, kitty" into the poison oak. We sent Granny's dog Rex into the poison oak to flush out the cat. Nothing. Rex came out of the vines and tried to jump up on me. I danced away from him and said, "No, Rex, no Rex." Greg looked again at the Uncle Roland gun. I decided to go back to the house to get the .22 rifle out of my car. I had lately been trying, without much success, to kill the groundhogs excavating my father-in-law's pasture. Marsha was waiting for me in the backyard. She told me that if I hurt the cat she would have me arrested. I told her to get the fuck away from me. I had never talked to anyone in my family like that. I was going to hell as fast as I could.

I walked around to the front of the house to see if the cat had come home. No one on the porch had seen it. I turned to start back toward the barn with the rifle.

Aunt Barbara touched me softly on the arm. "Tony," she said, "do you want your daddy and your uncle Lonnie to go out there and shoot the cat?"

"I'm a grown man," I said, as if that were an answer to her question.

Greg and I never did find the cat. We looked for it until almost suppertime, until long after we ever expected to see it emerge from the poison oak. It came back to the house only after everyone went home. Granny gave it a saucer of milk. The cat drank a few sips and walked away.

My father provided this story with what seems to be the proper ending. He went by Granny's the next morning and without fanfare shot the cat. While I still don't know if that was the best possible ending for this particular story, I admire its simplicity, its lack of modern ambiguity. I am neither pragmatic nor decisive nor lucky enough to tell a story like that.

My parents came from a South where spending good money on a dying cat would be considered a great foolishness, if not an outright sin. For better or worse, I grew up in another South entirely. In the South I know the cat is still in the poison oak. I am supposed to do something, but I'm not sure what. I go around telling anyone who will listen that I am from the country, but deep down I know it's a lie. I grew up on Gilligan's Island, in Mayberry, I'm not sure where. My *family* is from the country. They are waiting on the porch to see what I will do.

[The Quare Gene]

I do not like, have never liked, nor expect to like, watermelon. For the record, I consider this a private, dietary preference, not a political choice, neither sign of failing character, nor renunciation of Southern citizenship. I simply do not like watermelon. Nor, for that matter, grits, blackberries, cantaloupe, buttermilk, okra, baked sweet potatoes, rhubarb, or collard greens. Particularly collard greens. I don't even like to look at collard greens. But, because I am a Southerner, a North Carolinian of Appalachian, Scots-Irish descent, offspring of farming families on both sides, my family finds my failure to like the foods they like somehow distressing. Whenever I eat at my grandmother Ledbetter's table, my relatives earnestly strive to convince me that I am making a mistake by not sampling this or that, that I do not know what I am saying when I say no, that I should just *try* the greens, have just a little *slice* of watermelon, a small *bite* of canta-loupe, that I would eventually get used to the seeds in black-berries, the mealiness of grits, the swampy odor of greens boiled too long in a big pot. And, when I refuse, as I have been refusing with passion and steadfastness for as long as I could talk, they stare at me for a few seconds as if they do not know me, their mouths set sadly, then look down at their plates as if preparing to offer up a second grace. Then my grandmother says, "Tony Earley. You're just quare."

—⁂—

According to my edition of the *Shorter Oxford English Dictionary*, *quare* is an Anglo-Irish adjective from the early nineteenth century, meaning "Queer, strange, eccentric." Most dictionaries, if they list the word at all, will tell you that it is dialectical, archaic, or obsolete, an anachronism, only a mar-ginal, aging participant in the clamoring riot of the English language. But when spoken around my grandmother's table, by my parents and aunts and uncles and cousins, *quare* isn't archaic at all, but as current as the breath that produces it, its meaning as pointed as a sharpened stick. For us, *quare* packs a specificity of meaning that *queer, strange, eccentric, odd, un-usual, unconventional,* or *suspicious* do not. In our lexicon, the only adjective of synonymous texture would be *squirrelly,* but we are a close bunch and would find the act of calling each other squirrelly impolite. No, in my grandmother's house, when quare is the word we need, quare is the word we use.

Nor is *quare* the only word still hiding out in my grandmother's dining room that dictionaries assure us lost currency years ago. Suppose I brought a quare person to Sunday dinner at Granny's house, and he ate something that disagreed with him. We would say he looked a little peaked (pronounced *peak-éd*). Of course, we might decide he is peaked not because he ate something that disagreed with him, but because he ate a bait of something he liked. We would say, why, he was just too trifling to leave the table, and ate almost the whole mess by himself. And now we have this quare, peaked, trifling person on our hands. How do we get him to leave? Do we job him in the stomach? Do we hit him with a stob? No, we are kinder than that. We would say, "Brother, you liked to have stayed too long." We would put his dessert in a poke and send him on his way.

When I was a child I took these words for granted. They were simply part of the language I heard in the air around me, and I breathed them in. I knew that if I ran with a sharp object I might fall and job my eye out; the idea of jabbing my eye out would have sounded as foreign to me as French. My grandmother's table was the center of the universe. Only when I began to venture away from that center did I come to realize that the language of my family was not the language of the greater world. I was embarrassed and ashamed when my classmates at Rutherfordton Elementary School corrected my speech, but, by the time I entered college, I wasn't surprised to learn in an Appalachian studies class that my family spoke in a *dialect*. I had begun to suspect as much, and was, by that time, bilingual. I spoke in the Appalachian vernacular when I was with my family and standard English when I wasn't. This tailoring of speech to audience, which still feels to me a shade ignoble, is not uncommon among young people from this part of the world. In less generous regions of the greater American culture, the sound of Appalachian dialect has come to signify ignorance, backwardness, intransigence, and, in the most extreme examples, toothlessness, rank stupidity, and an alarming propensity for planting flowers in painted tractor tires.

—⚭—

THIS IS NOT some sort of misguided, Caucasian appeal for ethnicity, nor is it a battle cry from the radical left against the patriarchal oppression of grammar, but the fact is that, for me, standard English has always been something of a second language. I have intuitively written it correctly from the time I started school, but speaking it still feels slightly unnatural, demands just enough conscious thought on my part to make me question my fluency. When I am introduced to a stranger, when I meet a more showily educated colleague in the English department at Vanderbilt, when I go to parties at which I feel unsure of my place in that evening's social pecking order, I catch myself proofing sentences before I speak them— adding g's to the ends of participles, scanning clauses to make sure they ain't got no double negatives, clipping long vowels to affectless, midwestern dimensions, making sure I use *lay* and *lie* in a manner that would not embarrass my father-in-law, who is a schoolteacher from California. I try, both consciously and unconsciously, with varying degrees of success, to remove words of Appalachian idiom from my public vocabulary before the person I'm talking to decides that I'm stupid. Occasionally even my wife, whose Southern accent is significantly more patrician than my own, will smile and ask, "What did you just say?" I realize then that I have committed a linguistic faux pas, that I have unwittingly slipped into the language of my people, that I have inadvertently become "colorful." I'll rewind my previous sentence inside my head so I can save it as an example of how not to speak to strangers. I say, "What do you think I said?" Only inside the sanctity of Granny's house do I speak my mother tongue with anything resembling peace of mind.

—⚒—

I BEGAN thinking about the language I learned as a child, compared to the language I speak today, after reading Horace Kephart's book, *Our Southern Highlanders*. Kephart was a librarian and writer who, following a nervous breakdown, left his wife and children and moved to the mountains around Bryson City, North Carolina, in 1904. Although he traveled there initially to distance himself from human contact, he soon recovered enough to take an active interest in the world in which he found himself. An avid gatherer of information and a compulsive listmaker, Kephart spent the rest of his life compiling exhaustive journals and records detailing the geography, history, culture, and language of the southern Appalachians, a pursuit that resulted in innumerable magazine articles and two editions of *Our Southern Highlanders*.

Although Kephart had chosen the Appalachians over the deserts of the Southwest simply because it was the wilderness area closest to home, he arrived in western North Carolina at a particularly fortuitous time for a man of his particular talents. In the roadless hollows of the Blue Ridge and the Smokies Kephart found a people living largely as their ancestors had lived in the latter half of the eighteenth century, when the great Scots-Irish migration out of Pennsylvania first peopled the region with settlers of European descent. The hostile geography of the mountains had simply walled off the early settlers from the outside world and precluded, for almost a century and a half, extensive contact between their descendants and the greater civilization. "No one can understand the attitude of our highlanders toward the rest of the earth," Kephart writes,

> until he realizes their amazing isolation from all that lies beyond the blue, hazy skyline of their mountains. Conceive a shipload of emigrants cast away on some unknown island, far from the regular track of vessels, and left there for five or six generations, unaided and untroubled by the growth of civilization. Among the descendants of such a company we would expect to find customs and ideas unaltered from the time of their forefathers . . . The mountain folk still live in the eighteenth century. The progress of mankind from that age to this is no heritage of theirs.

Kephart was particularly interested in the English dialect he encountered in North Carolina, which he believed was closer to the Elizabethan English of Shakespeare or the Middle English of Chaucer, than anything that had been spoken in England for centuries. Because the Scots-Irish had spoken to, and been influenced by, so few outsiders, the language they brought with them from Scotland and Ireland, by way of Pennsylvania, had been preserved remarkably intact. Coincidentally, had Kephart come to the mountains a generation later, his research would have been by default less definitive.

Within a few years of his death in 1931, road-building initia-
tives, radio, and the Sears-Roebuck catalog began to open
even the darkest hollows of the Appalachians to twentieth-
century America. In just a very few years, the resulting cul-
tural homogenization turned the southern highlands into a
world vastly different than the one he discovered in 1904.

I have since learned that Kephart's research methods
were primitive by contemporary standards, and he was one
of the first purveyors of what have since become suspect
Appalachian generalities, but *Our Southern Highlanders* held
for me the power of revelation. Before reading the book, I
knew only that I had always been quare, and occasionally
peaked. I just never knew why. Kephart's work told me who
I was, or at least where I came from, in a way I had never fully
understood. All of the words I thought specific to my family
had entries in the dictionary compiled from Kephart's research of southern Appalachian idiom. And all of them—
with the exception of quare, which is a mere two hundred
years old—are words of Middle English origin, which is to
say anywhere from five to eight hundred years old. Although
most of the people I meet today wouldn't have any idea what
it's like to eat a bait, Chaucer would have.

Of course, a word of Middle English origin is a mere babe
when compared to the words of Latin, Hebrew, or Greek
etymology that constitute much of our language. The Latin

and Greek roots of the words *agriculture* and *barbarian* were old long before the primitive tribes of the British Isles painted their faces blue and grunted in a dialect resembling English. And, of course, no language is a static property; the life cycle of words mirrors the life cycles of the individuals who speak them. For specific words to fall out of favor and be replaced by new ones is the natural order of things; every language, given enough time, will replace each of its words, just as every population replaces the old with the young, just as every seven years the human body replaces each of its cells. The self-appointed guardians of English who protest that the word *celibate* means "unmarried" and not "abstinence from sexual intercourse" are wasting their time. "Sounds are too volatile and subtle for legal restraints," Samuel Johnson writes in the 1755 preface to his *Dictionary of the English Language*. "To enchain syllables, and to lash the wind, are equally the undertakings of pride." Understanding this, I am not advocating a return to eighteenth-century Scots-Irish dialect for the residents of western North Carolina. I am less taken by the age of the words of the Appalachian vernacular that found their way into my grandmother's dining room than I am by the specific history they hold.

The word *quare,* for me, contains sea voyages and migrations. It speaks of families stopping after long journeys and saying, for any one of a thousand reasons, "This is far enough." It speaks to me of generations of farmers watching red dirt turn before plow blades, of young men stepping into furrows when old men step out. It speaks to me of girls fresh from their mother's houses, crawling into marriage beds and becoming mothers themselves. It bears witness to a chromosomal line of history, most of it now unmappable, that led to my human waking beneath these particular mountains. If language is the mechanism through which we inherit history and culture, then individual words function as a type of gene, each bearing with it a small piece of the specific information that makes us who we are and tells us where we have been. My cousin Greg and I came down with the same obscure bone disease in the same knee at the same age. For us the word *quare* is no less a genetic signifier of the past than the odd, bone-eating chromosome carried down through history by one wonders how many limping Scots-Irish.

—⚹—

THE LAST time I remember talking to my maternal great-grandfather Womack, he was well into his nineties and our whole family had gathered at the house he had built as a young man along Walnut Creek in the Sunny View community of Polk County. When I tell this story, I choose to remember it as a spring day, though it may not have been, simply because I like to think that the daffodils in his yard were blooming. My grandmother had helped him plant them when she was a little girl. At some point, everyone got up and went inside, leaving Paw Womack and me alone on the porch. I was in high school, a freshman or sophomore, and was made self-conscious by his legendary age. He had been born in another century. His father had been wounded at Gettysburg. He was *historical*. He had farmed with a mule until well into his eighties. He never bought another car after the one he bought in 1926 wore out. A preacher's son, he had never uttered a swear word or tasted alcohol. He had voted for Woodrow Wilson. I felt somehow chosen by the family to sit with him; I felt like I needed to say something. I got out of my chair and approached him as one would a sacred totem. I sat down on the porch rail facing him, but I had no idea where to start. I remember his immense, knotted farmer's hands spread out on the arms of his rocker. We stared at each other for what seemed like a long time. Eventually I blushed. I smiled at him and nodded. He smiled back and said, "Who *are* you?"

I said, "I'm Reba's boy. Clara Mae's grandson."

"Oh," he said. "Reba's boy." If we ever spoke again, I don't remember it.

It seems significant to me now that when I told Paw Womack who I was, I didn't give him my name. My position as individual was secondary to my place in the lineage, his lineage, that led to my sitting on his porch. I identified myself as a small part of a greater whole. *Who are you?* I'm Reba's boy, Clara Mae's grandson, Tom Womack's great-grandson. *Where are you from?* Over yonder. *Why don't you like watermelon?* I don't know. I guess I'm just quare.

—ɷ—

Ironically, just as I learned, from Horace Kephart, to fully appreciate the history contained in the word *quare,* I also have to accept the fact that it is passing out of my family with my generation. Neither I nor my cousins use it outside of Granny's house unless we temper it first with irony—a sure sign of a word's practical death within a changing language. I tell myself that the passing of Appalachian vernacular out of my family's vocabulary is not a tragedy or a sign of our being assimilated into a dominant culture, but simply the expected arrival of an inevitable end. "Life may be lengthened by care," Dr. Johnson says, "though death cannot be ultimately defeated: tongues, like governments, have a natural tendency to degeneration." I tell myself that it is a natural progression for my children to speak a language significantly different from that of my parents, but the fact that it happened so suddenly, within the course of a single generation, my generation, makes me wonder if I have done something wrong, if I have failed all the people who passed those words down. Sometimes the truest answer to the question "Who are you?" is "I don't know."

A few years ago an ice storm splintered a large stand of pine trees on my grandmother Ledbetter's farm. When the broken timber was logged and removed, our whole family was shocked by how close the mountains were behind the ridge where the trees had stood. We all walked out the road past the barn to have a closer look, almost as if we had never seen them before. "These very mountains of Carolina," Kephart writes in *Our Southern Highlanders*, "are among the ancients of the earth. They were old, very old, before the Alps and the Andes, the Rockies and Himalayas were molded into their primal shapes." Young's Mountain, Rumbling Bald, Chimney Rock, Shumont, World's Edge, White Oak: my family has apparently always lived in their shadow. They preserved in their hollows and laurel hells the words that tell us better than any others who we are. Words and blood are the double helix that connect us to our past.

As the member of a transitional generation, however, I am losing those words and the connection they make. And by losing language, I am losing the small comfort of shared history. I compensate, in the stories I write, by sending people up mountains to look, as Horace Kephart did, for the answers to their questions, to look down from a high place and see what they can see. My characters, at least, can still say the words that bind them to the past without sounding queer, strange, eccentric, odd, unusual, unconventional or suspicious. "Stories," says the writer Tim O'Brien, "can save us." I have put my faith in the idea that words, even new ones, possess that kind of redemptive power. Writers do not write about a place *because* they belong there, but because they want to. It's a quare feeling.

[The Courting Garden]

We were engaged to be married, and the summer was lush with our courting. Days, I drove around in circles, waiting for evening. Evenings, we lay on the carpet beneath a twirling fan and planned the coming days. Outside, the moon rose, the dogs sang, and the cows waded through the towhead fog breathed out by the sleeping grass.

One night Sarah said, "Let's plant a garden."

And I said, because I was in love and would have agreed to any number of less reasonable requests, "I would love to plant a garden with you."

At the time we suffered the delusions with which God mercifully touches the betrothed. All we really knew of each other were the things we hoped to be true. During those courting nights we made up a world out of whole cloth and peopled it with our longings: we were patient and kind and devoted, and, in a moment, simply because we wished it, became gardeners of diligence and skill. Insects and weeds would bow before us, and rain would fall for fifteen minutes every afternoon. Vegetables would spring from the earth as symbols of our love.

It is ironic that a garden born in the euphoria of courtship provided our first intimation of the true nature of marriage: Sarah showed up at the appointed spot bearing a copy of *Square Foot Gardening,* and I met her wielding a mental engraving of my grandmother's perfect garden. Granny plants her vegetables in rows—long rows; I could plainly hear her saying, "Why Tony, don't you know a square foot of corn ain't worth fooling with?"

We faced off in the middle of a small piece of plowed ground in the corner of a hayfield. Sarah wanted to go by the book—she had, after all, purchased it for *us,* didn't I appreciate *that?*—while I considered the book a manual for treason. My family had been growing vegetables in North Carolina, in rows, for two hundred years. Around us lay shovels and rakes and hoes, heavy bags of fertilizer and small packets of seeds, but we could not agree even on how to start. Sarah's eyes filled up with tears. I knew what she was thinking, because I agreed with the thought: this does not bode well.

God saved us then, the first of many times, by revealing the mechanism that converts the enormous weight of individual expectations into the forward motion of marriage: we agreed, each against our better judgment, of course, to compromise. We planted our garden in rows—very short rows, but rows— that were at once faithful to the principles of *Square Foot Gardening,* but linear enough to show Granny. We dug into the earth then with purpose and vigor, vain with maturity and reason, content that the invitations waiting on the dining-room table could be posted in good faith.

We worked side by side the rest of that day, man and woman, Baptist and Episcopalian, beneath a beneficent June sun. We planted corn and beans and Irish potatoes, green pepper plants and Better Boy tomatoes; we planted basil and dill and oregano, and exotic lettuces whose names sounded more like minor characters in Shakespearean comedies than the primary ingredients of salads. We worked until a prodigal band of delicate freckles wandered across Sarah's nose, and the fragile writer's flesh covering my palms peeled away, re- vealing the red, embryonic skin of a man who works the earth alongside the woman he loves.

This was, of course, at the start of what has since come to be known as The Great North Carolina Drought of 1993. The days were brilliant and hot and dry, each identical to the day before it, and the day that would follow. Sarah and I lay tensely beneath the fan and whispered, *Did you hear that? Was that thunder?* June stretched into July, and July rattled toward August. The whippoorwills around the pastures marked the passing days, and the frogs along the thinning river chanted for rain. We stretched hoses from the house and watered the garden until Sarah's father returned one day from filling the horse trough and announced that the well was running dry.

As the ground hardened into red pavement, our garden naturally failed. Our herbs didn't come up at all, although for a few days our spirits were lifted by a troop of rogue morning glories that appeared in the square foot marked BASIL. The beans sprouted optimistically, but just as quickly stopped growing and bowed as if we had misled them. Our corn hunched awkwardly in the far corner of the garden, like thirteen-year-old boys whose radical tassel styles didn't quite make them feel better about themselves. Only the grass, which had been hastily flipped in order to make that corner of the hayfield at least *look* like a garden spot, made discernible progress. It righted itself, and set about repairing the scar that the drought and our good intentions had cut and burned into what had been perfectly good pasture.

In some ways, the drought was perhaps a blessing: because the conditions that summer were so quantifiably unfair, I did not learn for sure if my family's penchant for growing vegetables had passed intact to me. I don't know to this day, and I'm content with my ignorance. I take solace in the fact that I could still turn out to be a great gardener in the same way that I secretly believe I might possess the ability to throw an unhittable knuckleball. The unexamined life may not be worth living, but sometimes it allows you to live momentarily on planets more romantic and interesting than your own.

Sarah, meanwhile, turned out to be a woman of this earth. Often, when I arrived at her house in the evening, I found her scratching around in our garden, a rescue worker refusing to give up in the aftermath of unspeakable vegetable disaster. Sometimes I caught her sneaking a single glass of water from the house, which she poured into the ground around some plant that seemed incapable of making it through another rainless day. She grew angry when I told her that all was lost, and tried to lead her away. The drought that consumed our garden showed my future wife to be a woman of faith, and her faith, it's been my private blessing to learn again and again, is most often rewarded.

One night, when I arrived at Sarah's house for dinner, I found her at the sink washing a green pepper. "Where did you get that?" I asked.

"From the garden," she said.

"*Our* garden?"

"Our garden." She held up the pepper for me to see. It was darkly green, perfectly formed, flawless, a miracle. Its pulp was fragrant and juicy and sweet. Sarah chopped it up and added it to the spaghetti sauce simmering on the stove. We ate it, and it was good.

We married that October. The scripture we chose for the service was from John, chapter 15: "I am the true vine . . . you are the branches. Those who abide in me and I in them bear much fruit, because apart from me you can do nothing . . . This is my commandment, that you love one another as I have loved you." Our rings were engraved with grapevines. Father Murphy's homily, to our great surprise, compared marriage to a garden, one that will flourish only with faithfulness and care. My mother, who had seen our garden, remembers that her exact thought at that moment was, "Oh God, no." By then the only evidence that remained of our garden was as faint as the lines left on the earth by ancient roads, visible only in satellite photographs. Guests at our reception parked in the middle of it, and assumed, correctly, that it was a hayfield.

Weddings, of course, have less to do with being married than with the simple fact that it is best to begin the most arduous journeys surrounded by friends and wearing nice clothes. And while our journey together has at times been arduous, I have never regretted it. God has never failed to provide, in the midst of every drought, and from the most seemingly barren soil, the single, perfect pepper that, on finding it green at our feet, makes us glad we are traveling together. We bought our first house during the middle of a harsh winter, and found, come spring, that one whole side was covered with grapevines. At those moments we smile like spies from the same small country, on spotting the other in a foreign airport, each bearing half the secret we need for survival. We click our rings together and move on, watching the ground, toward whatever miracle comes up next.

[Ghost Stories]

I go to Louisiana at the end of the summer to look for ghosts with my wife. We drive down out of Tennessee, and down through Mississippi, taking turns at the wheel, the one not driving reading out loud to the other. The air conditioner in our old car is trying to die; we hold our hands in front of the vents, testing and imploring. We stop at the Wal-Mart in Hammond and buy a flashlight. The interstate dives out over Lake Pontchartrain toward New Orleans on the back of the world's longest bridge. In the middle of the causeway Sarah says, "I'm not sure I believe in ghosts." She is a seminary graduate. "I don't know why God would need them."

We have just passed a dead water moccasin. I wonder how

it got up onto the bridge. I say, "Maybe ghosts don't have anything to do with God."

Sarah says, "If they don't have anything to do with God, then I don't want to have anything to do with them."

To our right, small deserted-looking houses perch on pilings driven into small hummocks of something not quite land. The houses are tin-roofed, ramshackle, their windows screenless and gaping. To our left the blue lake spreads out like a new ocean. A long column of electrical pylons wades across the water and disappears into a thunderhead rearing up from beyond the horizon. When we pass underneath the heavy power lines, the pylons, for an instant, vanish behind the pylon nearest us. The day is hot and beautiful and we are married and going to New Orleans to look for ghosts, although, I think, just one will do.

I say, "You're not going to pray that we don't see any ghosts are you?"

"I don't know," Sarah says. "I might pray that nothing bad happens to us."

—⁂—

I HAVE WANTED to see a ghost since my sister died. I was a freshman in college; she was a senior in high school. She rolled our mother's car down an embankment draped with kudzu. This happened a few days before Christmas break. I went home without taking my exams. My sister lived a week on a respirator, her head bandaged so that only her mouth was visible, then she died.

I went back to school when Christmas break was over. One night I had a vivid dream: I was studying in my dorm room when the buzzer above the door went off. I went downstairs; the door to the phone booth was open; the receiver swung gently beneath the black phone. All these years later I can still smell the phone booth, the cigarette smoke, the body odor, the stale air inside the small room.

I said, "Hello?"

My sister said, "It's me."

I said, "It can't be you, you're dead, where are you?"

She said, "You're not going to believe this, but I'm in heaven."

I was a freshman in college, so I did not believe in God. I said, "Get out of here."

She said, "No really. I'm in heaven and God is a really cool guy. You'd really like him."

I felt myself believing, wanting to believe, growing conscious of something that had always been around me, something I needed, like the air. But I said, "I don't believe you," because I was afraid.

"Look," she said. "I have to go. I just wanted to tell you that everything is okay."

I thought I heard a voice in the background on the other end of the line, maybe somebody waiting for the phone. I called her name. I said, "Please don't go."

She said, "I can't talk anymore. I have to go now. Just don't worry about me, okay?"

And then she was gone. The phone buzzed in my ear.

That night, my mother dreamed the same dream.

—w—

"THE TERM *haunt* comes from the same root as *home*."— *Harper's Encyclopedia of Mystical and Paranormal Experience.*

—w—

THE DOORMEN at our hotel wear bermuda shorts and white gloves and braided jackets worthy of admirals. I am not sure whom I should tip, or how much. I keep my hand in my right pocket, a dollar bill clutched in my fist like a crucifix. From our room we can almost see the river, and we can almost see the French Quarter. We have two TVs on which to watch the Olympics, and a bidet, which seems to me now a marvelous invention. We go down to the lobby and ask the concierge if it's safe to walk to the French Quarter. It is our first time in New Orleans. We haven't been in town long enough to learn to call the French Quarter "the Quarter." The concierge smiles. "Absolutely," she says. She produces a map of the

Quarter from beneath her desk and draws big Xs east of Dumaine and north of Dauphine, making the Quarter more like an Eighth. "I suggest you don't go into these areas," she says, pointing at the Xs. Then she looks at us seriously. "And whatever you do, don't go into the cemeteries by yourself. Not even in the daytime."

—⟊⟊—

"ARE there ghosts in the Bible?"

"I don't know. I'll look it up."

—⟊⟊—

"NOW A word was brought to me stealthily, my ear received the whisper of it. Amid thoughts from visions of the night, when deep sleep falls on men, dread came upon me, and trembling, which made all my bones shake. A spirit glided past my face; the hair of my flesh stood up. It stood still, but I could not discern its appearance. A form was before my eyes; there was silence, then I heard a voice: 'Can mortal man be righteous before God? Can a man be pure before his maker?'"—Job 4:12–17

—⟊⟊—

THE TALL hotels of Canal Street lean out over the French Quarter like rich, thin men throwing dice. We pass electronics store after electronics store, each staffed by Indians with identical thick mustaches. On Bourbon Street we find ourselves wandering simultaneously through a Disneyfied past, and some dark future where all that we knew as good has gone twinkling off into rapture. For every window demurely shuttered behind a graceful wrought-iron railing, for every small alley that at its end reveals a secret garden, a door swinging open frames a naked woman writhing in a smoky darkness. We stare in the window of an art gallery where a sixty-eight-thousand-dollar sculpture of Charlie Parker's disembodied head plays a golden saxophone, and moments later pass a club whose loud sign promises LIVE SEX ACTS WITH MALES AND FEMALES. In the middle of the barricaded street an old woman in a blue dress sings "Amazing Grace" so slowly that the tune is almost unrecognizable and each note becomes a small song worthy of a quarter. A few steps beyond the old woman four frat boys in an open-air bar, drunk on zombies, shout the lyrics of "Wild Thing" into a karaoke microphone, their heads bobbing stupidly, out of time like fouled pistons. We walk past two small boys, brothers, taps tacked to the bottoms of their small, black sneakers, who stop clicking long enough to tell us they dance five hours a day and make lots of money; we lean over and read small signs screwed to the sidewalks reminding revelers not to dump their drinks into the storm drains because the sewers flow straight to the river; we walk through air-conditioned cold spots, loitering in front of the small shops that sell film and Mardi Gras beads and feathered masks and T-shirts proclaiming I GOT LAID IN NAWLINS. A pleasant-looking woman who says she is a school teacher raising money for Meals on Wheels attempts to write us a ticket because we are not partying hearty enough, and we give her a dollar. We wander into what we assume to be a Southern folk art gallery because the sign in its window says SOUTHERN FOLK ART, but find ourselves staring instead at a collection of human skulls. Sarah grins and points down St. Peter Street, where I see a full moon climbing into the black, tropical sky. "Oooo," she says. "Scary." We walk back to the hotel and through the lobby and smile at the concierge. We go upstairs and drape ourselves in white, crested robes, climb into a bed the size of a small fiefdom, turn out the lights, and watch the Olympics on TV.

—ⵎⵎ—

"ENGLISH psychical researcher Harry Price was among the first to use modern technology in his ghost investigations . . . Price put together a ghost-hunter's kit that included felt over-shoes, steel tape measures, a thermometer, a still camera, a remote-control movie camera, fingerprinting equipment, a telescope, and a portable telephone."—*Harper's Encyclopedia of Mystical and Paranormal Experience.*

—◊◊◊—

It is not easy being a parapsychologist, at least a legitimate one, in New Orleans. The city is filled with charlatans and shysters and weirdos who make livings pretending to be parapsychologists and mediums and ghost busters; even people in the city's chamber of commerce bait tourists into visiting, and paying to visit, "haunted" buildings you know for a fact have never housed a ghost; witches and warlocks and voodoo priestesses and devil worshipers regularly cast spells at you because they don't like the questions you ask; close-minded people with chips on their shoulders regularly lie to you, invite you to investigate properties they know are not haunted, simply hoping you will fake your findings, make up a ghost *story,* just so they can denounce you as a fraud. "Look," Marty Revenant says, a little wearily, "these things are either in the house or they're not. You can tell that as soon as you walk in the door."

Revenant is a parapsychologist, a professional paranormal investigator. We meet him in the bright morning. He wears bermuda shorts and a light, cotton shirt and boat shoes. He carries a flip phone, which he excuses himself often to answer. He could be a podiatrist on a Saturday. His associate Susan Smothers is good-looking and friendly. She is from Ohio. She seems as normal as he does.

Revenant says he studied electrical engineering at Tulane

and parapsychology at UCLA; he has been a parapsychologist, a *scientist*, for twenty-three years. He appears regularly on national television — *Unsolved Mysteries* and *Sightings* and specials on A&E. ABC recently flew him to Los Angeles, not to be on a television show, but to investigate a studio whose paranormal activity was driving crews off the job. Hotels all over the country hire him to investigate the rooms in which guests refuse to stay overnight. He would probably swim the Mississippi to make a charlatan take the word *parapsychologist* off his business card. He wants nothing more than to document, with irrefutable, scientific evidence, the existence of ghosts, but therein lies the single most frustrating part of his frustrating job. "We just don't have the technology yet to accomplish what we want," Revenant says, looking a little pained, like a petroleum engineer forced to use a dousing rod, or a microbiologist wielding a magnifying glass in the middle of an epidemic. He and his team can chart the magnetic field of a haunted house with highly sensitive magnetometers, they can minutely plot the tiniest fluctuations in temperature and barometric pressure and thermal radiation, but ghosts aren't simply magnetic fields or weather or atomic energy; they are something *else*, an anomaly for which the proper instrument of measurement doesn't exist. The width of the gap between knowing that ghosts exist — and Revenant knows, he's *seen* them, he *sees* them all the time — and proving to a cynical world, once and for all, that they do, accounts for the note of resignation in his voice, the slight shrug, when he leans back in his chair and says, "That's why we still have to use psychics as an investigative tool."

I tell Revenant about my sister. "Ah," he says. "She manifested herself to you in a dream state."

—⁂—

"Enter GHOST."—*Hamlet*, Act I.i

—⁂—

Revenant and Susan take us to a little theatre on St. Peter Street. Revenant says it is the most haunted property in the most haunted city in America. He tells us it's where seventy years ago an actress named Catherine hanged herself after sleeping with a director and then not getting the part; where another actress, Carolyn, laughing with friends after a show in which she starred, fell from the balcony overlooking the courtyard and broke her young neck; where Sigmund, the cranky, dead stagehand, unplugs spotlights just before shows are supposed to open, and shoves actors onstage before their cues; where Alejandro Benagas, who is very, very old, who over the years has haunted almost every theatre in the French Quarter until only this little theatre is left, sits in the same seat on the right side of the balcony and ignores patrons holding that ticket until they leave in exasperation and ask an usher to remove the handsome man in the strange, formal clothes; where five black men sitting in the stackroom disappear into the air and scare the hell out of a stagehand; where six children, none of whom died there, live in the children's theatre, in the good energy left by live children laughing, where they are watched over by Carolyn, who loves them; where only five dead children lived until last year, when Carolyn found Stephanie, raped and murdered and lost, wandering the streets of the French Quarter and brought her in to live with the others.

—⁕—

"PRIESTS USUALLY have no effect at all," Revenant says. "If you get a really hostile entity, you can bring in a hundred Catholic priests and the Pope and it still won't go anywhere."

I say, "Entity? Doesn't that imply a . . ."

"Yes," Susan says excitedly, leaning across the table toward us, "a *consciousness.*"

—⁕—

FROM INSIDE the children's theatre, through the windows looking out onto the courtyard, we can see the balcony from which Revenant says Carolyn, laughing, fell and broke her neck. The theatre is closed for the off-season. Dust motes hang almost suspended in the thick, hot air, in the lazy light drawing the shapes of the tall windows onto the floor. I walk across the stage, holding my hand out in front of me. I am looking for a ghost. "The children are in here," Revenant says. "They're all around us." On top of five stacked chairs I feel a cold place in the air. It covers exactly the width of the seat. Revenant closes his eyes and for a moment goes off somewhere. He inhales sharply, once. "It's Carolyn," he says. I try to feel an entity, a presence, but what I feel is a cold place in the air above a stack of chairs. A phone rings in the theatre office, and in an instant the cold place disappears; around my hand it is hot summer in New Orleans inside a closed-up, empty room. "They're gone," Revenant says. And that is all I know to tell you.

—⁋—

"Dost thou work wonders for the dead? Do the shades rise up to praise thee?"—Psalms 88:10

—⁋—

On the way to lunch, near Jackson Square, I buy a Diet Coke at a Lucky Dog stand. Portrait painters and tarot card readers try to make eye contact with us from the shady spots beneath the old trees. Dead Creole planters duel in the garden behind the cathedral, only I can't see them. A black guy levitates before a crowd of tourists. An ice-cream man yells, "Ice. Yo, Ice."

Sarah says, "Marty seems anti-Christian."

I say, "No he doesn't. He's a scientist." I raise the cold, plastic bottle to my lips.

"NutraSweet," she says. "Phenylalanine. You know that stuff's going to kill you."

"Something's got to kill everybody," I say.

Sarah whispers, "Poison. Poison."

———∿∿———

I say to the waitress, "Does Chef Paul still cook here?" I have seen Chef Paul cook on TV.

"Oh no," she says, "but he comes in a lot."

"Really?"

"Sure. Sometimes people see him."

———∿∿———

In a small, gated courtyard off Toulouse Street, we join a tour led by Brandon Osborne. Brandon writes a column called "Ask the Psychic Investigator" for a paranormal newsletter. We meet a young-looking woman from Maryland and her teenage daughter, and an American petroleum engineer from Indonesia, on vacation with his wife and two young sons. The older boy is wearing a Shaquille O'Neal T-shirt; the younger one has glasses and an unusual accent. We are look-ing for ghosts together. Brandon's T-shirt identifies him as our PARANORMAL GUIDE. He is tall and handsome and clean-cut; he looks like a Mormon missionary. Like Revenant and Susan, he does not seem odd. He shouts so that we can hear him over the heat pumps whirring in the courtyard. He tells us that each of the properties we will visit is actively haunted, that one time a ghost attacked a woman in one of the tour groups, that another time forty-eight people on the stage of the little theatre saw Alejandro Benagas watching them from his seat in the balcony. "Wow," says the younger boy. He sounds vaguely English. Brandon says, "Be sure and speak up if you begin to feel even a little strange." He points at his eyes. "Psychically, you learn not to trust these so much." I tell the woman from Maryland that already that morning I have felt a cold spot in the air. She nods and says, "Really?" The wife of the petroleum engineer glances at Sarah. The pe-troleum engineer says, "Here we go."

—⟋⟍⟍—

IN THE little theatre, Brandon tells Catherine's sad story, and asks if anyone can find the place where she hanged herself. The woman from Maryland takes a tentative step forward, then marches directly to the spot. "Here," she says. "I think I'm getting something here."

"She's *good*," says Brandon.

I sit beside the petroleum engineer in the back of the children's theatre. The rest of the group is walking slowly through the room, their arms waving like tentacles, their hands swimming through the thick air, searching for cold spots. They look like an interpretive dance troupe recruited in a mall. "You know," the petroleum engineer says, nodding at his sons, "we let them choose. They could have gone to the zoo."

—⁓—

BRANDON leads us to the bar in the Shalimar Indian Cuisine restaurant. He tells the group about an entity they call the Sikh. A drawing of the Sikh, made by a psychic sketch artist, hangs in the tour company's office. The Sikh's calling in life, Brandon says, was guarding a wealthy woman. He attached himself to the mother of the Shalimar owner while passing through New Orleans. She does not mind him, although he makes the rest of the family nervous. Brandon takes us upstairs to the dining room to show us the corner where the Sikh is most often seen. The room is still crowded from the lunch buffet. The diners look up from their Chicken Tiki Masala, read Brandon's T-shirt, then smile at us.

"Oh man," says the petroleum engineer.

—⁕—

In a small café on Toulouse Street Brandon shows us where a secret door that is no longer there opened out onto an alley that is no longer there. The café was a speakeasy during Prohibition. He shows us the mysterious, unsigned painting of a flapper that was uncovered during a recent renovation. We move among the cabaret tables in the deserted hall, searching for cold spots. On the darkened stage I can't find Arthur, the trumpet player and compulsive gambler who died of a heart attack playing off his debts to the speakeasy's owner, nor can I find the two musicians who died here in a fire and who, along with Arthur, make up the club's prank-playing, equipment-moving trio of dead jazzmen; nor can I find the Italian, who is surly and vain and ill-tempered and wears a tuxedo with a red flower stuck in the lapel and parts his black hair down the middle, who manned the speakeasy's secret doorway until he was shot dead at his post for sleeping with the boss's wife. Brandon speaks of the Italian affectionately, like an eccentric friend he humors to keep out of trouble. He was the first ghost Brandon ever saw. In spite of myself, I no longer think I am going to see a ghost at any of these haunted places. I am starting to feel a little desperate. I want to believe in the Italian. I don't want to live in a world where people die and are gone away forever. I want to leave New Orleans with a sign. I stand on the spot where the

Italian was shot dead for his sins. I look around to make sure no one can hear me. I blush, feel the rims of my ears grow hot, then whisper, "Come out, you wop bastard."

—⟋⟍—

WE CHECK out of our tall hotel and move into the French Quarter. We check into Room 110 of the Dauphine Orleans, which is notoriously haunted. "Oooo," Revenant says when we tell him. "Good luck in there." His investigative team encountered an entity in the room so malevolent that one of his psychics refused to go inside. They almost had to force the door in order to enter. While they were setting up their equipment, something jerked the curtains off the window. The manager of the hotel decided to join the frightened psychic out by the pool.

Sarah crosses herself before stepping over the threshold into our room. I say, "I wish you hadn't done that."

—⟋⟍—

"NOT EVERYONE who goes to a haunted place experiences paranormal phenomena. It is theorized that only individuals with certain psychic attunements or emotional states are receptive."—*Harper's Encyclopedia of Mystical and Paranormal Experience*

—⟋⟍—

WE ARE told that the Dauphine Orleans was originally a whorehouse. Wealthy Creole planters kept their Octoroon mistresses there for the days they rode into town to drink and gamble and screw. Our room is very nice, although it doesn't have a bidet. The brick walls are original; the exposed beams bear the tool marks of the slaves who hewed them out of live oak logs. Revenant sends his associate Jim Scranton over to scan the room for entities. Jim is the youngest member of Revenant's investigative team. Once, during a particularly spooky hotel investigation, he wheeled and snapped a Polaroid picture of an ice machine when it dropped a load of cubes into its bin. Now all the other investigators call Jim Ice Boy. Unlike everyone else on the team, Jim has no particular psychic ability. He is trying to develop it, and to that end has quit drinking. Lack of psychic ability, he tells us, is a considerable handicap for a paranormal investigator. "In other words," he says, removing a magnetometer from his briefcase, "I'm basically blind." Jim and I take turns walking around the room with the magnetometer. The room reveals a fairly high level of residual energy, but nothing remarkable. I say, "So there's nobody in here with us?"

"I'm afraid not," Jim says. "Sorry."

"But they could show up any time."

"Oh sure," he says. "Definitely."

—⁓—

I SAY TO the maid coming out of Room 109, "Do ghosts live in our room?"

"Shoot," she says. "Ghosts live everywhere."

—⁂—

SARAH IS watching the women's three-meter springboard diving finals and eating a bag of Doritos. "I know what went wrong," she says. "We forgot our felt overshoes."

—⁂—

SARAH IS peacefully asleep. I am trying to stay awake. I have left a lamp on so I can see. On one wall is a bad painting of a flamingo and an ibis wading in a marsh. Perched on a limb above the larger birds is a small, incongruous cardinal. The cardinal is the state bird of North Carolina. The bar manager at the Dauphine Orleans is from North Carolina. Sarah and I are from North Carolina. The bar manager's hometown has a paper mill I can smell when she mentions it. The cardinal is watching me. I do not want to be watched over by the official bird of my home state. I do not want my bartender in New Orleans to sound like my aunt back home in the mountains. I don't want to hear any more ghost stories. I don't want to go to sleep yet. I want to see Creole shades step out of the walls and fight with long pirate knives. I want to hear a Greek chorus of Octoroon courtesans scream in French for them to stop. I want to see the dead living. And when I pray for God to banish them from our room, I want to hear in my voice the clarity of belief, not the twang of my fallen Baptist accent.

—⁓—

Sarah says, "Good morning."

I say, "Did you hear . . ."

"Soap dish," she says. "The soap dish fell in the shower."

I say, "Do you think . . ."

Sarah says, "I think the soap dish fell."

—⁓—

We leave New Orleans and drive to St. Francisville, a small town north of Baton Rouge. We check into The Myrtles, a plantation house bed-and-breakfast whose ghosts are famous for showing up in photographs made by the plantation's guests. The plantation looks just right: the long, white drive curves from the highway through a large yard of ancient live oaks bearded with Spanish moss. The house is two hundred years old, with a deep porch and wide double doors and tall windows of distorted, antebellum glass. Behind the house is a small fountain and a formal garden filled with blooming crepe myrtles. From a gazebo surrounded by a small, snaky moat we stare through a spider's ornate web at the garden and the fountain and the old house darkening in the twilight. The spider is black and yellow, the size of a small dog. Cicadas scream around us in the dark woods. "Oooo," Sarah says. "Scary." I look into the moat for water moccasins. I feel optimism rising inside me like the moon.

—⟋⟍—

I ASK the woman who gives us our key why our room is called the Twins' Room. She says because it has two beds.

—⟋⟍—

TWO COUPLES from Baton Rouge pull up into the parking lot in an Astro van. They are drinking bourbon out of LSU cups. One of the men is wearing round glasses and a golf shirt. He looks like a lawyer. The other has the evil mustache of a stock car racer. The lawyer's wife is tall and blonde and pretty. The stock car racer's wife is short and round and talks constantly. The stock car racer takes a key and goes upstairs to use the bathroom. He comes back downstairs and says that something is holding the door closed. I clinch my fist and whisper to Sarah, "Yes!" We run upstairs with the stock car racer and the stock car racer's wife, with the lawyer and the lawyer's wife, with the lone waiter from the restaurant, and the owners' nephew, Ty. The waiter climbs onto the roof from another room and tries the bathroom window. Ty walks over to the bathroom door and opens it. We see the waiter staring at us through the window. The stock car racer says, "Oh, wait a minute. I was trying the wrong door." Ty says, "Get off the roof."

—◊◊—

"A MAN who wanders from the way of understanding will rest in the assembly of the dead."—Proverbs 21:16

—◊◊—

TY TELLS US The Myrtles has been rated by the Smithsonian as the most haunted house in America. He shows us the step on the main staircase, the seventeenth from the bottom, on which one owner of the place died after being shot on the porch by a stranger; he shows us the mirror in the hallway in which claw marks appear, no matter how often the mirror is resilvered or the glass replaced; he tells us about the dead groundskeeper who has been videotaped walking the grounds, about the strange man who dreamed so vividly of The Myrtles, which he had never visited, that he begged his way into the house and spent a frantic hour talking in the dining room to a dead little boy named Tom; he leads us to the two photographs of the house, taken by his aunt, which reveal the transparent form of a woman in a long skirt and a head rag passing between the main house and the kitchen; he points at the figure in the photos and says, "That's Chloe." He tells us Chloe was a house slave, a kitchen girl, a beautiful woman who was visited often in the night by her master; how, when the mistress of the house learned of the liaisons, she demanded that her husband banish Chloe to the canefields; how Chloe was caught eavesdropping during the conversation, a sin for which her ear was cut off, how the mistress then allowed her to stay, because she was no longer beautiful; how one day Chloe baked a cake and poisoned it with oleander leaves; how the mistress ate it and gave a piece to each of her little girls; how all three of them died. Ty tells us how the other slaves, when they heard what Chloe had done, hung her in rage and grief. He tells us that late at night guests often hear little girls laughing and bouncing a ball in the hallways, how the son of the current owners, when he was four years old, talked constantly of his "little sisters," when, in fact, he had no little sisters, and how he once said to his mother, "Mama, make my little sisters get off the ceiling." He tells us about the men sitting in front of the service station across the road who saw two little girls in long dresses chase a hoop to the end of the driveway and vanish. He tells us how Chloe still wanders the hallways and grounds of The Myrtles, looking after the ghosts of the little girls she did not mean to kill.

———ᴂ———

I GET UP and sneak out and wander the grounds whispering, "Chloe? Chloe?" until I get so scared I can no longer make myself stay outside. I hurry upstairs, climb back into bed, grateful that I am married, that I do not have to sleep in the Twins' Room at The Myrtles by myself. I start to ask Sarah if she is awake, hoping the question itself will wake her, when I hear myself call her Shelly, which was my sister's name.

Later, I hear the low love moan of the lawyer's wife rising from the room next door. In the morning I hear her say, "Oh, honey, I have *got* to quit drinking. I drink too *much.*" At breakfast the lawyer doesn't have much to say. The stock car racer and the stock car racer's wife swear they heard footsteps in the hallway outside their door, show us a balled-up Kleenex they found that wasn't there when they went to bed.

—⚬⚬—

THIS CHRISTMAS Shelly will have been dead longer than she was alive. I was eighteen when she died. I imagine she is still seventeen. If we could see each other again I think she would say, "What happened to *you*?" and I would say, "My hair fell out."

—⚬⚬—

SARAH IS wearing the straw hat in which she likes to travel. She smiles. "Well," she says, "nothing bad happened to us."

I say, "You're right. Nothing bad happened to us."

The air-conditioning in our old car feels cool in the new morning. I hold my hand in front of the vents, testing, wanting to believe it will work. Our next stop is Tuscaloosa, Alabama, where I went to graduate school, where I stayed one year too long and almost drank myself into pitch blackness, where at the last minute I veered instead toward the brightest light I could see, which was Sarah. She opens the atlas and positions it in her lap. I am filled suddenly with hope. I don't think I will ever die. We are looking for ghosts, but, I think, a good story will do. Sarah points to Tuscaloosa on the map. She says, "Okay, here we go." We drive away, beneath the twisted oaks, and at the highway encounter five buzzards squatting studiously over a mangled carcass. I blow the horn and turn right, into the haunted world.

[A Worn Path]

Rock Springs, the church I attended as a boy, sits on the spine of a ridge surrounded by the blue mountains of western North Carolina. The church roll contained forty names, though on an average Sunday only half that many attended the service. I was related to almost everyone who went to church there. The small congregation, though sincere in its hymn-singing, boasted little musical talent. My mother, who took piano lessons for a single year as a girl, was by default our music director and pianist. The choir consisted of five women, two of whom were almost deaf. Mom's hymn selections grew by necessity from the small patch of common ground shared by the songs she knew she could play on the piano and those the congregation was capable of singing. The first time I attended the Episcopal church in my hometown with a girlfriend, I was shocked by the complexity of the melodies the organist played, by the sheer, tuneful competence of the singing. Until then I don't think I knew it was possible to worship God in cadences and keys actually indicated in a hymnal.

In the years since I left, Rock Springs has added air-conditioning and a sound system and a fellowship hall, but has changed little in one important way: the congregation still sings out of green, dog-eared copies of the 1940 *Broadman Hymnal.* Though I heard the songs in the *Broadman* sung well only once a year, on Homecoming, the third Sunday in May, when the church overflowed with visitors and our musical shortcomings were hidden inside a joyful noise, they have always been the songs I love best. I would be hard-pressed to recall even a single sentence from the hundreds of sermons I heard growing up at Rock Springs, but I can sing from memory at least one verse from each of the hymns we sang from the *Broadman.*

The congregation of Rock Springs was a dignified, reserved bunch, unlike the shouting Pentecostals with whom they shared their small community and were loathe to be confused. It was rare, even, to hear someone at our church call out Amen during a sermon, except during the summer revivals, when a visiting minister preached every night for a week and the Holy Ghost sneaked in through the open windows and moved silently through the thick, hot air. During revival even the most staid members of the congregation allowed themselves to be overcome by the spirit at least once. Spiritual renewal was as necessary to the people of Rock Springs as breathing, but was, like the private conversations they shared with their husbands and wives, a part of their lives of which there was no polite way to speak. Once revival was over, the men and women I knew best, fortified by grace for another year, simply went back to work. And if, before the time for revival came again, they suffered through crises of faith, or began to doubt the rightness of the paths they had chosen, I never heard them say.

Because the people of Rock Springs were by nature circumspect, we sang "Just As I Am," the traditional Baptist hymn of invitation, only during revival week, when the public displays of religious emotion likely to be sparked by the song were corporately sanctioned. On bright Sunday mornings, we found the hymn's power to break down the walls hiding our secret hearts simply inappropriate, like hand-clapping in time to the music, or speaking in tongues. Even during revival week Mom selected it cautiously, like a doctor prescribing a purgative whose toxicity is almost as dangerous as the disease it treats.

One revival night when I was eight years old, the words

and music of "Just As I Am" mixed in the darkness of my sin-
ner's heart with the strange preacher's sermon, and flamed
suddenly into Jesus Christ's great love. I clutched the pew in
front of me, torn between going to the front of the church,
where our pastor waited to receive those of us called by Jesus,
and staying put because I was afraid. I didn't know that my
struggle was apparent until the couple standing beside me
stepped back so that I could reach the aisle. I wandered to the
front of the church, through music in which God lived and
spoke, conscious of how small I was, before God and in the
eyes of the people I had known forever. Our pastor leaned
over, and I whispered into his ear that I wanted Jesus Christ to
be my savior. I was not baptized that summer only because
the visiting pastor, whose name and face and words I can no
longer recall, convinced my parents that I was too young to
know what I was doing.

Four years later, when I reached twelve, the age of ac-
countability, when Baptists believe God begins keeping track
of their children's sins in His ledger, I wanted no part of
Jesus or revival. I wanted everybody to leave me alone. The
first night of revival that year another visiting minister, whose
shape and message I also forgot years ago, preached a sermon
that called the undiluted spirit of the living God down upon
our heads. When, at the end of the service, my mother struck
the first notes of "Just As I Am," the congregation heaved a

collective sob and moved en masse down the aisle to the altar. Mom abandoned the piano, leaving the congregation to sing without accompaniment; they sang the first verse over and over from memory because they had left their songbooks in the pews. I found myself sitting alone in the last pew in the back of the church. I was the only person in the congregation who did not go forward to dedicate, or rededicate, my life to Jesus. Again I felt the fierce pull of God rising up from the hymn, the siren song of Jesus' perfect love, but this time it infuriated me. God and Rock Springs had not wanted me before; I would not make the mistake of offering myself to them again. What I remember most from that night is the sight of both of my grandmothers on their knees, crying and begging me to join them at the altar. They were afraid I would die without being saved, that I would spend eternity crying out in hell for God to save me. I did not join them, though as they reached out to me and called my name, joining them was the thing I wanted to do most. I closed my eyes and shook my head back and forth until the congregation finally stopped singing and the preacher dismissed us out into the night.

—⚋⚋—

MY GRANDMOTHER Earley was a tiny, fierce woman, capable equally of great love and great hate. She loved my father, her baby, exorbitantly, but swore on his wedding day that she would never forgive my mother for marrying him. And she didn't. She stopped attending Rock Springs before I was born because someone insulted her in the churchyard; she did not return until I was in high school. But she was also a devout Christian, acknowledged in the community to be a woman to whom God spoke. People brought her questions for God to which they especially needed answers. When she was troubled she prayed without ceasing, until God's will became clear in her mind. If she could not get an answer, she ran everyone out of the house, as if their presence interfered with God's signal beaming down, and climbed into the closet, where she prayed for hours in the dark and the quiet. Other times she went off into the woods along the creek and knelt in the laurel until God gave her a word she could repeat when she opened her eyes.

Granny Earley spent most of her life on a red, upland farm, a mile down the ridge from Rock Springs, frustrated by my grandfather's lack of ambition. Paw-paw Earley found God's provision for them enough, but his willingness to settle for their life as it was infuriated her. Their farm was, literally, through no fault of Granny's, a one-mule operation. They kept chickens and a pig and a milk cow; they fed the livestock and themselves on what they grew in the fields. They worked a small patch of cotton to earn money for the things they could not grow or make. My father and uncles worked with them in the fields until they were old enough to leave home. Because the farm was small and the ground poor, they were never able to save anything that made them richer, or even better off, than they had been the year before. Granny prayed constantly to keep their small world intact.

One fall day when my father was a boy, the wind turned bitter and cold several weeks early. When the sun set behind the mountains, the air bristled with frost. Granny hadn't picked the green beans hanging on the vines in her garden. The beans she canned each fall were the only green vegetables the family had to eat until the following spring, but that year the early frost caught her unprepared. She simply ran out of time. The sky was clear and purple above the black mountains when the family came in from the fields. Paw-paw brought in an armload of wood and started a fire in the stove. Granny paced around and around the living room. She could not accept losing her beans. She told Paw-paw she had to talk to God. She walked out of the house and down across the pasture toward the woods in the twilight. She came home several hours later, stiff and shivering with cold, and announced that God said he would give her one more day.

The next morning Dad watched his breath steam in front of his face as he dressed in his room. His window was intricately jeweled with frost. Outside, the frozen world sparkled in the new sun and the grass crunched under his feet as he walked with Granny up the path to the garden. Everything in the garden was dead, had been burned by the frost, except Granny's beans. The bean rows drew vivid green lines across the white field. Granny picked every bean in the garden that morning and canned them that afternoon. That night another frost settled onto the ridgetop and killed the stripped vines. "Now let me tell you something," my father says, "I *saw* that."

—⁓—

WHEN I visited Granny and Paw-paw Earley during the summers when I was small, I slept on a folding cot in their living room. From the living room I could look into their bedroom. Every night I watched Granny turn out the light and get down on her knees beside the bed. She crossed her hands on the mattress and laid her head on her hands. She prayed silently, without moving, for what seemed like hours. I tried to stay awake to see how long she prayed—my prayers never took longer than a minute to complete, and I wanted to know by how much I was failing—but I always fell asleep before she said Amen.

One night I woke up out of a dream and saw Granny still on her knees beside the bed. I didn't know how much time had passed, but felt as if I had traveled a great distance through the secret middle of the night. Paw-paw snored softly. The windows were bright with starlight. The black outlines of the thick, summer trees were sharp against the sky; the rich, country dark rattled with the rhythmic sawing of insects. Granny, I knew suddenly, was dead. I have never been more sure of anything. I was terrified, and didn't know what to do. I had never seen a dead person. I wanted to wake up Paw-paw, but was afraid to pass by Granny in the dark. I opened my mouth to call out, but the darkness gobbled up whatever small sound I thought about making. I clasped my hands together underneath my chin and prayed, forming the words inside my head, but not saying them out loud, "Please God, don't let Granny be dead. Please don't let Granny be dead." I had prayed no more than a minute when Granny slowly straightened up. She put her hands flat against the mattress and stiffly pushed herself to her feet. She turned and looked into the living room at me. Her face glowed faintly in the darkness; it changed and moved as I squinted at it. The black holes of her mouth and eyes twisted into a smile. I jerked the sheet over my head, terrified by what I had done, by the power I had called down out of the night with a prayer.

—◆—

I DECIDED to kill myself during an ice storm one Sunday night my sophomore year of college. I was failing all my classes, and was about to be fired from my campus job. My sister had died the year before, and I could not understand how it was possible that I still lived. I could not imagine seeing the end of the day that faced me. The pine trees outside my dorm bent beneath a great, frozen weight. Occasionally a limb let go with a sharp, ripping crack. Sleet hissed against my window. I could not get warm, nor could I go to sleep. I climbed out of bed, got dressed, and shoved my paperback copies of J. D. Salinger's books into the pockets of my parka. I told my roommate I was going for a walk and would be back soon. I planned to climb the small mountain that rose up behind the soccer field, dubbed "suicide ridge" by the cross country team, remove my parka, and lie down underneath a tree.

The road to suicide ridge led by the college chapel, which loomed darkly in the icy trees to my left. The building was modern and A-framed and Presbyterian, constructed out of stone and light-colored wood. I had never been to a service there. As I walked past, I turned sharply on my heel, climbed the icy steps, and went inside. I didn't think about what I was doing. I don't remember thinking anything at all. The sanctuary was warm and quiet. I sat down on a pew on the right side of the aisle, about halfway to the front of the church. I unzipped my parka. The tall, wooden cross floated in front of the stone wall behind the altar, lit from behind by fluorescent bulbs. As I stared at the cross a great rage bloomed inside me. I cursed God out loud. I shouted. I called him every vile name I could think of. I challenged him to fight me or kill me right then.

At that moment I heard a noise, a small wooden thump, behind and above me, like a surreptitious footstep. God was hiding in the choir loft. I ran to the back of the church and stumbled up the steep, wooden stairs. The choir loft was empty, but on the back wall I saw a door cut into the woodwork, almost invisible, like the opening to a secret passageway. I heard another thump, this time behind the door. God was trying to get away. I jerked the door open, stepped through it, and pulled it shut behind me. I have never been in a darker place. The light switch I found did not work. Off to my left somewhere I heard a single, muffled knock, like that made by a knuckle tapping once on a wall. I felt my way along the wall until I found a small door. I turned the knob and stepped into a room as dark as the hallway I had just left. I stood still and listened. The only sound was that of my own breathing, but I also knew that God was in there with me. On good days I know it still. I imagined him laughing at me, and I cursed him for hiding. I stepped forward, groping in the dark with my hands, trying to find him. Each step I took I expected to touch his chest, to feel his indifferent heart beating beneath my fingers; I expected to touch his ancient, hoary face in the darkness. Only on bad days do I consider the possibility that I manufactured him from the electricity of psychosis. That night I discovered and explored four black rooms, two on each side of the hallway. All night long the building creaked and thumped; all night long I chased God through the darkness in a rage. I chased him until exhaustion finally squeezed the anger out of my body. When I stopped cursing and began to cry, I went back through the secret door into the choir loft, and down the stairs into the sanctuary. I returned to the pew on which I had sat hours earlier. The cross still floated above the altar. I zipped up my parka and lay down. I woke up just before daylight. I walked back up the aisle and stood outside the chapel and looked at the world. The temperature had risen during the night, and most of the ice had melted from the trees. I walked back to my dorm through a steady rain and a thick fog. I climbed into bed and fell asleep.

—⁊⁊—

FRIENDS HAVE asked me to be the godfather to their daughter, Jessie. While I am touched by her parents' faith in me, I feel particularly unqualified for the job. I was an angry, resentful, unforgiving Baptist. I attended an Episcopal church the first time only to impress a girl, and went back because I loved the forbidden papal theatricality of the service. I loved the smell of incense as much as I loved the smell of beer, and probably for the same reasons. The sad truth is that I do not like Christians much, particularly when they congregate. I think that whenever two or three people gather in God's name, it's only a matter of time until they start trouble. The sight of half a million Christians praying together in Washington, D.C., filled me with dread. I've found the churches I've attended to be filled with people who are as ill-tempered, hypo-critical, judgmental, and divisive as I am, and I'm invariably as disappointed in them as I am in myself.

And now I am about to be a godfather, charged with lead-ing a child into the faith, which proves, if nothing else, that God has a sense of humor. Jessie is a beautiful child, five months old, who beams at the world as it passes; a dog trot-ting by or a stranger leaning in fills her face with brightest joy. She knows nothing but good in the world, and I spend a lot of time wondering about what I should tell her. I suppose I should tell her first that I believe. I still doubt most every-thing, including the motives of all organized religions and the journalistic integrity of the gospels, but I do believe that I am watched over by a God who loves me, who kept me alive, for reasons known only to him, all the years I wanted to die. I will tell her I have no idea what God wants me to do, only that every time I arrive at a desperate place, usually of my own devising, a path opens up in front of me, whether I have prayed for a path or not. I will tell Jessie that I have come to have faith in the path opening up, that I keep going because I believe. I will tell her that when I remember I say thank you. So I suppose I will tell my goddaughter she should always say thank you and please.

When Jessie is old enough I will tell her about the dark places I have been, the ways I hurt myself and other people because I was angry. I will tell her of the years I tried to

convince myself that I was an atheist, how I made fun of
Christians with the single-minded zeal of a preconversion
Saul. I will tell her about the night God pulled me out of the
ice and into his house. I will tell her to drink beer only mod-
erately, and never around boys. Jessie lives in the mountains
in Tennessee, and I like to think we'll walk along the ridges
near her house until we come to a place where we can see a
long way, maybe even all the way to the blue mountains of
North Carolina. I will tell her that there are people out there
who will love her and people who will hurt her, that sometimes they will be the same person. I will tell her how Granny
Earley loved me and tried to turn me against my mother at
the same time. I will also tell her that I rarely find the strength
to forgive the people who hurt me, that I nurse and enjoy a
multitude of small hatreds, and that I am ashamed for it. On
the way home I will show her poison oak, and tell her how in
our part of the world the leaves of all the poisonous plants
grow in groups of three; I will tell her that in our part of the
world all the poisonous snakes have triangular-shaped heads.
(The lone exception, the coral snake, is also unmistakably
marked.) I will tell her that these things are miracles, at once
reminders that we live in a fallen world, and proof of God's
great love. I will tell Jessie that as we walk through the world,
even along the dangerous paths we have chosen for ourselves,
God worries about where we put our feet.

[Granny's Bridge]

In 1953, when he was sixteen years old, after the waitress at the diner on the road to Lake Lure had broken his heart, my father ran away from home. He and two of his buddies left the red dirt farms and red mud roads of Polk County, North Carolina, and lit out for Florida. Florida, at that time, was inhabited mostly by girls—girls in bathing suits who drank fresh orange juice and danced for Jackie Gleason and skied twelve at a time behind the big boats at Cypress Gardens—and my father and his buddies had a plan: they were going to leave their overall-wearing, fertilizer-toting, God-I-hate-listening-to-Ernest-Tubb-on-the-radio days unspooling behind them on the highway; when they crossed the Florida line, they were going to be Men, cool as cats in sunglasses and pegged pants and pink shirts, with ducktails out to here. They'd get jobs—as lifeguards, maybe—and to meet girls, why, all they had to do was open the door and step into the sunshine.

When my father and his buddies turned up missing, Dad's ex-girlfriend (my mother, temporarily supplanted in his affections by the waitress at the diner on the road to Lake Lure) stepped forward and revealed where they had gone. She had overheard them talking about their plan in Buster Wilson's store. My grandmother Earley's heretofore unfocused anger and worry and grief darkened and whirled into a spitting cloud of hysteria capable of blowing in only one direction: Florida. She boarded a bus pointed south, dragging the mother of Buddy Number One along with her.

—✺—

GRANNY EARLEY was born Odessa Searcy in the Rock Springs community of Polk County in 1904. While you could see the beginnings of the rest of the world from any high place in Polk County, finding a way down from that high place lay beyond the reach of most of the people who lived there then. Rutherfordton, the nearest town big enough to be honestly called one, lay twenty miles away by dirt road, an all-day trip by wagon, and the town itself, although tethered to the world by a railroad track, was hardly a beacon of civilization. By the time I grew up there, in the sixties and seventies, the population had grown to only three thousand people. Despite her poverty and isolation, Granny grew up keenly aware that *possibility* lay beyond the mountains, that something else was out there, something she couldn't even name. She possessed a sharp, occasionally cunning, intelligence, as well as an undirected, almost pathological ambition that ultimately proved unsuitable, if not damaging, to the vessel that contained it. That she rarely made it out of the five square miles in which she lived all but a few days of her seventy-eight years was the source of a lifelong, choleric frustration. "She had the fire in the gut," my father says, "but spent her life on a red dirt hill, cussing the ground."

Granny's parents, Romeo and Sarah Searcy, were devout Baptists and semiliterate farmers who never lived farther than a sick mule or a dry summer away from disaster. "At my deth," her mother wrote in a note she placed in the family Bible, "this Bible is odssa give bie hear mother with hear love frome mother." They pulled Granny out of the one-room school at Rock Springs after five years, convinced that, as a girl, she knew all she needed to know. When she was thirteen or fourteen years old, they sent her to Spartanburg, South Carolina, to work in a textile mill, but soon found out that the mill sponsored square dances on Saturday nights and made her come home. Back in Polk County, Granny chose the best of the limited avenues she saw open up before her:

she married a good-looking man. Charlie Earley was small but extraordinarily strong for his size, and was afraid of nothing in this world except buying on credit. One Sunday when she was eighteen, the day the marriage license they had secretly acquired was due to expire, my grandparents sneaked away after church and got married. Later that afternoon, one of Granny's sisters caught my grandfather with his hand inside my grandmother's blouse and told on them. ("He was playing with my breasties," is the way Granny described it.) When Granny refused to renounce the man I came to know, forty-something years later, as Paw-paw Earley, my great-grandmother Searcy "took to the bed" and said she was going to die. Granny, however, held her ground, and after several days my great-grandmother decided she wasn't going to die after all, got out of bed, and lived another forty years.

During the time he courted my grandmother, my grandfather worked as a tenant farmer, and hired out for wages at sawmills and the occasional liquor still. He also brought to the marriage a set of contradictions that seemed specifically designed to fuel in my grandmother a sporadic fury that lasted fifty-six years: while he was a good, honest man and capable of prodigious feats of labor and strength, he was at the same time profoundly unambitious. After they were married, Paw-paw refused to buy a place of their own, because doing so would have required him to borrow money. Instead, he and Granny moved from one tenant shack to another, until she stopped cooking and threatened to leave. Hungry, he borrowed money from an uncle and bought a small, nominally productive ridge-top farm, where he worked for the rest of his life with little discernible effect. "I used to get so mad at him I'd just beat him with my fists," Granny told me before she died. "I'd beat on him until he'd grab my hands and say, 'Now, look here. That's enough, Mama.'" He farmed with mules until the late 1950s, when my father, after graduating from high school, took a job in a textile mill and bought a tractor for the farm.

By the time I was in high school, Granny's ambition had hardened and soured into a kind of sad conniving. She walked and talked and acted the way she imagined a rich woman—a lady of society—would. For years, she dyed her white hair black, before eventually edging, near the end of her life, toward an odd, chemical auburn. She mixed and matched her clothing into color combinations that would have appeared startling on a tropical bird. She wore extravagant hats and elaborate costume jewelry and stalked up and down Main Street, making scenes in department stores. Encountering her in public without warning could be like wandering into a costume drama without knowing what it was about. Even in the last moments of her life, she pretended to be a person not entirely herself. In the emergency room, shortly before she died, the doctor attending her attempted to hand my mother Granny's purse. Granny, however, who never forgave my mother for marrying her baby boy, refused to let go of the strap. She looked my mother straight in the eye and told the doctor, "I've never seen that woman before in my life."

——

WHEN MY father ran away from home, my grandmother was forty-nine years old, still at the peak of her stamina and ability, but, knowing Granny, I imagine that she had already looked ahead and seen the point at which the road she traveled started inexorably downhill. Her two older sons had already moved away, and even if my father returned to Polk County safely, she must have realized, he was sixteen years old and would not stay home much longer. Paw-paw was still contentedly scratching away at his small patch of dirt, and showed no signs of developing the desire and initiative to attempt anything grander. Granny must have felt the world constricting around her, growing even smaller than it had always been. Perhaps this is the desperation that caused her to board the bus in Rutherfordton as a wild woman, a force of nature, incapable of hearing reason; perhaps all she was after were the two years she had left in which one of her children would still live in her house.

I wonder if she was thinking about any of this as the bus rolled into Spartanburg, past the mill where she had worked as a child, or if she was still overcome with grief at the thought that she would never see my father again. At what point did her hysteria subside into the drone of the bus engine and the hum of the tires, into the realization that she was surrounded by strangers traveling who knows where, and on what urgent errands? At what point did she finally look out the window and discover that she had passed into a new country, where nothing she laid eyes on could have been newer if God had minted it fresh, moments before? Most of all, I wonder what must have gone through her mind when she stepped off the bus in Jacksonville, and realized for the first time that Florida was a *state,* that Jacksonville by itself contained more people than she had seen in her whole life, that she had about as much chance of finding her son as she did of finding any of the nameless things that would make her happy.

—m—

SOMEWHERE IN South Carolina a few hours earlier, Dad and Buddy Number Two had begun to sing "Oh, Mine Papa," which made Buddy Number One so homesick that they had to put him out in Columbia and buy him a bus ticket home. The cost of the ticket took the better part of their combined cash. Dad and Buddy Number Two had just enough money left to make it to St. Petersburg, where they were arrested for vagrancy. Dad was sitting on a park bench in the sun when the cruiser pulled up. Buddy Number Two's father wired them bail and gas money.

They beat Granny home. The boys returned to school, both ashamed and heroic. Dad reconciled with my mother, who, years later, pregnant with me, found herself face to face, in an obstetrician's office in San Antonio, Texas, with the former waitress at the diner on the road to Lake Lure. They spoke civilly, but did not become friends. My grandmother, aside from the occasional day trip to visit relatives in upstate South Carolina, never again left the state of North Carolina.

The last time I saw Granny at home, I slipped easily into the role I had played opposite her many times before: I was the sensitive young man who wanted to be a writer; she was the woman looking back over her life from the vantage point of accumulated experience. She told me how, years before, while traveling, she happened to come upon the most magnificent bridge. It shot over the water so far she could barely see the other side. It was so high in the air she could hardly breathe as she crossed it. Off in the distance she saw a huge ship steaming toward port, and the bridge was tall enough for the ship to pass under it. Beyond the ship lay the ocean it had crossed. She told me that crossing that bridge was the grandest thing that had ever happened to her.

Not until much later did I realize that the bridge she described was the Cooper River Bridge in Charleston, South Carolina, and that she had been on her way to Florida to look for my father when she saw it. She did not mention that she was traveling with the mother of Buddy Number One, that she didn't know where she was going at the time, or that people snickered about that adventure behind her back for years. Instead, she chose to tell me, from what she must have considered an inadequate array of choices, that she had once seen a sight so extraordinary that she had become extraordinary by seeing it. In an alchemy of will, she took a bus, a bridge, and a failed journey and transformed them into the culmination of a life. It wasn't lying, exactly, but rather burnishing memory until it looked like hope. It was her voice crying out, "Here I am! Here I am!" even as it grew fainter and fainter and finally crossed out of earshot.

[Tour de Fax]

We were not your typical Concorde crowd. Randy Brouseau was a bounty hunter and bail bondsman from New Orleans. Mike Sandobal was a cook at a bar and grill in New Jersey. Mike and Randy and forty-six other people had won seats on the plane in a contest. I had talked my way onto the plane as a reporter. We stood on the tarmac at JFK and stared at the Air France plane on which we would be passengers during an attempt to set the speed record for sub-orbital circumnavigation of the planet. Our Concorde had the slightly dingy, souped-up look of a fast car a few years beyond bank financing. A Starsky and Hutch Torino, maybe, or a Chevelle Super Sport. It was a '78 model, and smaller than you would think.

A guy with slick hair and a double-breasted, reflective suit walked by us, scratching his ear with a walkie-talkie. The airport was under a security alert. The newspapers were filled with foreboding. The angry buzzing of terrorists had been detected close by. A hurricane hovered over the Atlantic as if deciding something. Nobody on the tarmac talked about suicide bombers and killer storms, but it was hard not to think about them. The security guy's suit changed colors in the light. Kyle Petty, the race car driver, stepped warily into the sun. He was one of our celebrities. It was time to board. "I can't believe I'm doing this," Mike said. He had never been on a plane before.

Randy leaned into my face. "Hey, man," he said, "do you know what a coon ass is?" Big veins stuck out on his neck. He had forearms like Popeye, and looked a little crazy.

I said, "A Cajun?"

"Naw," he said, "it's the little brown spot under a raccoon's tail."

Workmen pulled the gangway away from the plane and replaced it with a gangway that bore the words AIR FRANCE on each of the steps. A magnetic-looking sign prominently featuring the logo for Coors Light, our corporate sponsor, had been stuck incongruously on the fuselage, near the plane's sharp nose. If Arthur Helios, who organized the attempt, was Christopher Columbus, then the Coors Brewing Company was Queen Isabella. The French airline, the American brewery, and the entrepreneur had been joined in temporary alliance by an independent marketing firm. Columbus, sailing today, would need a marketing firm. In early press releases, the plane had been referred to as the Silver Bullet, a Coors trademark that apparently did not fly with Air France. By the day of the flight the plane had metamorphosed without explanation into the Coors Light Concorde. The original flight plan had called for it to make its first refueling stop in Lisbon, but at the terminal we found out we were landing instead in Toulouse, where the Concorde had been built. You could sense on all sides the great weight of seas recently parted; the air was sweet with the freshly faxed smell of detente.

I said to Randy, "*Laissez le bon temps roulez.*"

"Damn right," Randy said. "We going to fly around the world."

New York–Toulouse 3:20:02

Arthur Helios seemed too big for the airplane. His head brushed the ceiling of the cabin when he stood up straight. His shoulders reached from overhead compartment to overhead compartment. His personality probably would not have fit inside a smaller container. He produced a big declaration every time he opened his mouth. He spoke only in complete sentences, and most often in the declarative.

On the ground in New York he said, "I am the leading consumer advocate in aviation there is, period. I personally eliminated the forty-four-pound baggage limit for overseas travel. I couldn't care less about getting my name in the papers." In the itinerary he had mailed to all the passengers before the flight, he called the flight "the most exciting aviation event since Lindbergh crossed the North Atlantic." On board the Coors Light Concorde he was the biggest bear in the forest. "This plane only discriminates against two classes of people," he said. "The poor and the tall."

The Concorde, I found out, is considered luxurious because it is fast and the service is good, not because it is comfortable. I had to stand up in order to operate my tray table without hitting my knees. It was difficult to place my arm on the armrest without touching my seatmate, Laura, whom I had just met. She was also a reporter. We squeezed into our seats while Dave Brubeck's "Take Five" played on the PA. The flight attendants, male and female, were elegant and good-looking and solicitous. They seemed genuinely glad to see us, which was disconcerting. The uniforms of the female attendants had been designed by Nina Ricci. "That's another reason to hate the French right there," Laura said. The five journalists on board were seated like acolytes in the rows behind Helios. He split the port side of Row 1 with his fiancée, Betty. Betty was a tall, good-humored woman who seemed pathologically immune to big declarations. During the flight the journalists on board gradually came to be more and more like her: depending on the length of the writing assignments awaiting us back home, each of us gradually stopped writing down everything the big man said.

Retired Apollo astronaut Tom Stafford, our other celebrity, along with his wife, Linda, sat across the aisle from Helios and Betty. Stafford earned their seats on the flight with pull: he convinced the United States Air Force to allow an Air France plane chartered by a brewery to land on its base at Guam. Kyle Petty and Felix Sabates sat behind the Staffords in Row 2. Petty drove the Coors Light Pontiac for Sabates's NASCAR racing team. He boarded the plane like it was a bus taking him to a job he didn't particularly like. A gang of Floridian marketing guys filled the seats behind Petty and Sabates. It is hard to say how many seats: two marketing guys and a six-pack rapidly become a crowd. The marketing guys wore Rolexes the size of sundials, and polo shirts with the names of golf courses stitched above their hearts. They called Helios "Big Art," and used the word *party* as a verb. They laughed and sang and shouted, a little too loudly, like pirates in a movie musical. A handful of Coors executives sat behind the marketing guys. They were uniformly young and tan and buff. They wore T-shirts and diving watches and khaki shorts with lots of pockets. They did not seem happy with their seat assignments and kept mostly to themselves.

The attitude of the Concorde in flight is slightly nose-up, a fact of geography which means everyone seated behind you is also seated beneath you. Only Row 2 separated Laura and me from the best address on the plane. The rear compartment, where the contest winners were seated, seemed to be at the bottom of a long hill. After ten or twelve hours together in the thin, exclusive air of the forward compartment, Laura and I began to feel married. We shared cologne-scented moist towelettes and clinked our champagne glasses together and rooted around under the seats for each other's shoes. We stayed home most of the time and did not visit much. The rear compartment began to feel like the other side of the tracks.

We headed east over the Atlantic at 11:49:10 on a Tuesday morning. If we landed in New York by 8:30:12 Wednesday evening we would be able to say that only astronauts had traveled faster around the earth. The standing record had been set by the same airplane flying westbound in 1992, on a Helios-organized dash to commemorate the five-hundredth anniversary of Columbus's landing in the New World. Tickets for that flight cost around thirty thousand dollars a pop. For this trip Helios sought corporate sponsorship and spared himself the headache of selling seats. "There were two records and I already had one," Helios said. "What else could I do?"

We broke the sound barrier at 12:03 with no perceptible change in the way the plane flew. The Machmeter on the forward wall of the cabin simply went from .99 to 1.0. The moment was greeted by a smattering of tentative applause from the rear compartment, and an ironic cheer from the marketing guys. The director of the documentary film crew hired by Helios was not satisfied with our enthusiasm and goaded us into reliving the moment once more, this time with feeling. On his cue the marketing guys yelled like frat boys at the big game. The Coors guys waved their Coors baseball caps and held cans of Coors Light above their heads. The contest winners whooped dutifully, although only a handful of them were on camera.

We went to Mach 2 with less fanfare at 12:23. We were traveling faster than some bullets, twice the speed of a spoken word, more than ten miles above the ocean. I realized that I would probably never travel farther above the earth, or with greater velocity, than I was at that moment. I imagined the feeling to be not unlike having God tell me the exact second I reached middle age. I watched the Machmeter after that as if it were a heart monitor. Eventually our speed would drop below that of even the most carefully chosen word, and the ordinary sounds of our lives would catch up and find us and buzz around our heads. Outside the window I could clearly see the curvature of the earth. The sky was a delicate pale blue; immediately above us it began to curve and darken into the violet of space. The Machmeter read 2.02. For the moment I felt absolutely, perfectly safe.

Lunch began with canapés and champagne, followed by lobster salad with a julienne of mango pear, tournedos in peppercorn sauce, a potato croquette with truffles, slivered almonds, carrot and spinach subric, a salad, assorted cheeses, fresh fruit salad, and petits fours. The flight attendants wore blinking, battery-powered buttons shaped like Coors Light bottlecaps. The chief steward's button blinked beneath his white tuxedo like a visible heart. Laura and I hovered over our trays with our menus until we identified everything. We pointed eenie-meenie style at the bottles of wine offered us. Anything that came in an airtight container we stowed in our bags to take home as souvenirs. Laura was a light eater, so I finished off her beef. She nibbled at my cheese. In the rear compartment Mike, with a ravenous professional curiosity, ate everything he could get his hands on, even things he didn't like. He figured it would be his only shot at real gourmet food. By the time the flight attendants cleared our trays, we were only twenty-three minutes away from landing in Toulouse.

Without the Machmeter I could not have guessed the

moment we broke the sound barrier, but slowing to sub-
sonic speed produced in me a vague physiological sense of
disappointment, as if velocity were a euphoria from which
my body only unwillingly withdrew. France spread out suddenly below us, a flat, melancholy grid of green and brown
fields beneath a nondescript sky. Toulouse from the air looked
like a planned community outside Atlanta or Charlotte. The
houses were stuccoed and roofed with red tile; the small yards
were dabbed with the suburban blue of swimming pools. The
narrow roads outside the airport were lined with parked cars.
Hundreds of people clutched the wire of the hurricane fences
surrounding the airport, waiting, I realized, for us. They separated from the fences when we passed overhead, and waved
their arms as if we had come to rescue them. Hundreds more,
maybe thousands, waited for us at the terminal behind a security fence. Many of them had probably worked on the Concorde during headier times.

"My God," Helios said as we taxied in, "I hope we're getting
video of this."

He commandeered the plane's PA system. "Ladies and gen-
tlemen," he announced, "if you want to know why I do it, this
is why I do it."

The crowd behind the fence cheered as we descended to the
tarmac; we waved back like astronauts. Randy screamed and
pumped his fist in the air when he stepped onto the gangway.

Mike stepped out of the plane as if looking for his shadow. He did not *feel* like he was in France; only the strange cars and trucks parked on the tarmac made France look different from New Jersey. At the bottom of the gangway Helios addressed a mob of reporters in perfect French. Tom Stafford stood beside Helios, squinting into the television lights. He had commanded Apollo 10 and the Apollo-Soyuz mission, and retired from the air force a three-star general, but nobody asked him anything. He gradually began to inch away from Helios and look around for somewhere else to go.

We did not go through customs, in France or anywhere else. When we arrived back in New York, our passports would bear no evidence of our journey. We were led into an empty terminal and upstairs into a private lounge. A model of the Toulouse airport sat on a table. It was the only thing in the room to look at. The passengers gathered around it and took pictures. They posed in front of it with Kyle Petty.

Petty had read most of Elmore Leonard's *Riding the Rap* on the way over from New York. He was worried because he had brought along only two books for the trip. "I'm gonna have to find a store," he said. "I'm afraid I'm going to run out of stuff." He doesn't like to sit still without something to do. He collects first editions—Graham Greene, Hemingway, Eudora Welty—and reads them on airplanes. Thursday he would fly from New York to New Orleans for another promotional appearance. Friday he would fly from New Orleans to Michigan, where he would race on Sunday, blow an engine, and finish last in a field of thirty-nine cars. "You know how it is in high school," he said in Toulouse. "I didn't read shit."

We spent an hour and sixteen minutes on the ground. We sniffed at a table of hors d'oeuvres and sipped orange juice. The urinals in the men's room were visible from the door of the women's room. We accepted this as evidence of Gallic culture. On the way back to the plane Randy whistled at a tall woman in a miniskirt. Mike smiled and shook his head. At 4:25 P.M. New York time we took off into the French twilight. At 5:10 the marketing guys began to sing, "If you're happy and you know it, clap your hands."

Toulouse – Dubai 3:13:52

In the air our world condensed into the shape of an airplane. Perhaps at sixty thousand feet you lose some unnamed sense, which you maintain at lower altitudes, of belonging to the earth. The Mediterranean below us was an idea of which we had to remind ourselves, not a reality to which we belonged. Laura and I studied our menus as if we were hungry, but did not look at our maps.

An hour and fifteen minutes out of Toulouse, Helios announced that the United Arab Emirates had withdrawn its permission for us to fly at supersonic speed through its air-space. The projected drop in velocity would add forty-four minutes to our flight time and probably cost us the record. He did not take the news well. "The United Arab Emirates is essentially a sandpile consisting of Dubai, Bahrain, and Qatar, a bunch of countries none of us would want to live in if we had a choice," he said over the PA. "I basically want to get out of Arab airspace as fast as we can and not deal with these bastards again." The marketing guys hooted and slapped each other high fives. They yelled, "All right, Big Art." The Coors executives stared straight ahead without expres-sion, brave men facing the loose cannon they had just paid for. "In other words," Helios said when he returned to his seat, "they're feudal savages with too much oil money to spend."

A flight attendant appeared, like a UN envoy, bearing a tray of hot towels. It is a fact of nature that setting or not setting speed records does not seem so important once you drape a hot towel over your face. The steward followed, pushing a cart of bread. Laura and I shrugged and opened our tray tables and settled in to eat. Several courses later, Saudi Arabian officials miraculously approved a course and speed change that would allow us to cross the Kingdom at Mach 2. Super-sonic travel is usually permitted only over oceans. Barring un-foreseen delays, the Saudi gift meant the record would be a lock. "Boy," Helios said, calmer now, "this is suspense city." I looked down and realized I had champagne, Diet Coke, red wine, Coors Light, bottled water, and hot tea on my tray all at once. The rich, I realized, were different from you and me only in their unlimited access to beverages. For a moment I was intensely happy.

The temperature in the cabin increased noticeably over Saudi Arabia, even though we were fifty-eight thousand feet above the desert. I cupped my hands against the glass and stared out the tiny window into the most profound darkness I had ever seen. I could tell, although I can't explain how, that we were no longer flying above the sea, and that the land below us was empty of anything save the primordial heat. I hoped there was someone down there to hear the shockwave chasing us through the middle of the night. Part of the thrill of going really fast, I suppose, is having someone else know you are going really fast.

Dubai flared on the horizon, bright as a fire. There had been no gathering up of lights and highways and houses to prepare us for the sight of a city at night. A city simply appeared in the void. The wide, deserted boulevards ran out into the desert and stopped. We landed at 3:40 A.M. local time, dinnertime the day before in New York. The temperature was 96 degrees, down from a high of 120 the previous afternoon. Concordes have no air-conditioning once the engines power down. We were sweaty and miserable by the time the gangway was attached to the plane and the doors opened. The marketing guys sniffed their armpits.

The plane was surrounded on the tarmac by mustachioed soldiers carrying automatic weapons. A pair of airport officials covered the Coors Light logo with a cloth. Islamic law forbids the advertisement of alcohol, although the duty-free shops in Dubai are the cheapest place on earth to buy liquor. Good scotch costs three dollars a quart. Rolexes, real ones, can be had for five hundred bucks. People fly to Dubai from all over the world simply to shop at the airport. The billboards on the side of the bus we boarded for the short ride to the terminal advertised Ferraris. "Man," Kyle Petty said, "you ain't going to see that back home."

The terminal looked brand-new, as ornate as the cake at a bad wedding. It was the gift, we were told, of a generous prince. Once inside, we weren't allowed near the duty-free shops. An outbreak of shopping fever might have endangered the record. We were hustled instead through a maze of gleaming corridors to another private lounge. Armed guards were posted at the doors. In the men's room a small crowd gathered to study the Middle Eastern–style urinal. It was a hole in the floor, with foot pads on either side of the hole. "It's so you don't have to lift your robes," Kyle Petty said. We nodded and lined up behind it. The stonework around the hole was deli-

cate and ornate. The Western-style toilets and urinals on either side of it remained unoccupied.

Dubai–Bangkok 3:37:51

At 9:30 P.M. New York time, the sun blinked on over the Indian Ocean as if operated by motion detector. It was darkest
night one minute and bright morning the next. We saw three
sunrises and sunsets in two days. "Boy," said Helios, "this is a
hell of a lot of fun." We were forty-four minutes ahead of the
pace that promised to land us in the *Guinness Book of World
Records*. Helios was more excited about breaking the official
eastbound record of 36:08:34, held by Alan Paulsen, the CEO
of Gulfstream Aviation. We would beat Paulsen's mark by
almost five hours. "I remember watching the Queen Mary
and the Queen Elizabeth sail out of New York, and everyone
on the dock wished they were the ones leaving," he said. "I
love being a guy in a home office doing what the CEO of a
major corporation can't do with unlimited resources."

Tom Stafford slept across the aisle behind a black blind-
fold. *Lost Moon,* Jim Lovell's account of the Apollo 13 mission, lay open in his lap. Stafford himself had lost the moon.
The lunar landing module hadn't been ready by the time
Apollo 10 flew. Neil Armstrong, the commander of Apollo 11,
became the astronaut whose name everyone remembers.

The flight attendants began lowering the shades against the

midmorning sun. It was bedtime back home. For a time even the marketing guys were subdued. Kyle Petty tore through a borrowed *Sports Illustrated*. Randy prowled the rear compartment, looking for somebody to talk to. He said we were going too fast for him to sleep. "You get to do more in this life if you're going fast," he said. "If you don't get there first, the other bail bondsmen get the money. That's the way it is. You gotta get on down the road. You gotta *go*." Randy wore a Harley-Davidson T-shirt adorned with a particularly belligerent-looking eagle. His favorite bounty-hunting tactic is following the car of a bail jumper to a traffic light, and bumping it from behind when it stops. When the bail jumper gets out of the car, Randy goes after him with a pair of handcuffs. "I'll take the ass-whupping," he said. "Give me my money. Wouldn't you take an ass-whupping for a couple thousand dollars?"

A low field of cumulus clouds floated over Thailand as if tethered there. The shadow of each cloud lay distinct and motionless and cool on the ground beneath it. It was almost noon, local time. Steep, thickly forested mountains sprouted wildly from the rich valleys. The valleys were terraced with rice paddies up to the feet of the mountains. A four-lane, unfinished highway ran in a straight line to the horizon, through a wide swath of jungle, as if the horizon itself were a destination. "Laura," I said, "wake up. We're not in Kansas anymore." A golf course was crammed between the runways of the Bangkok airport. A foursome stood beside their carts in the middle of a fairway and watched us land. The shadow of the Concorde slid quickly over them, like that of a pre-historic bird, and then they were gone, just like that, out of sight behind us. Women draped garlands of fresh flowers around our necks when we entered the terminal. They led us to a private waiting room. An announcer over a tinny loud-speaker said, "Welcome to Thailand. Land of Smile."

In the waiting room six teenage girls in native costume per-formed a traditional Thai dance. The music seemed much too loud. It sounded like an AM radio being tuned. "Man," Kyle Petty said, "who decided this stuff *ever* sounded good? Did you ever think about that?" Five of the girls scattered flower petals around the feet of the sixth, whose role in the dance ap-peared to be that of a goddess. On a television set behind the dancers, an American weather report played on a BBC news program. We were about as far from home as we could get without leaving the planet. The people I cared about were as distant as they ever would be. I had never been in a position to think that before. My heart filled with acute, generic long-ing. I called Sarah back home to tell her I loved her. It was one o'clock in the morning back home; Sarah was asleep and never quite understood who I was. I hung up and wrote her a sentimental postcard that embarrassed us both when it ar-rived at our house two weeks later.

Randy grew impatient waiting to board the plane. He thought screwing around in airport waiting rooms was going to cost us the record. He stood beside the gate and scolded us for boarding so slowly. "Let's go, let's go," he said. "We got the need for speed. We got the attitude for altitude. Let's do it. Let's do it."

Rice paddies and golf courses soon spread out beneath us. A wide, brown river snaked its way into a brown harbor filled with boats. The brown of the harbor lightened and disappeared into the blue of the sea. We banked left and went to Mach 1 with the coast of Thailand still visible below.

Bangkok–Guam 3:01:29

I hung my garland of flowers from the air-conditioning vent above our seats, the Coors Light Concorde equivalent of a pink, plastic flamingo in a small, suburban yard. It was three o'clock Wednesday morning in New York, but in the small country in which we lived, I was no longer sure what day it was. Almost everyone on the plane slept. The shades were pulled tight. The cabin lights glowed faintly. A few miserable-looking passengers stared up with the secret faces insomniacs rarely have to present to the world. The flight attendants moved silently up and down the aisle, touching the back of each seat as they passed. They smiled down on us, like parents, whenever we opened our eyes. Kyle Petty closed a copy of *Atlas,* the Air France magazine, and for the first time switched off his reading light. Laura opened her eyes every time I moved. I could not get comfortable, but tried to keep still.

The sun set at five A.M. In the Pacific twilight our bodies began to rouse themselves for a morning breaking on the other side of the world. Some of the passengers stretched and stirred and ordered coffee. When they opened their shades to peek at the sunset, the darkened cockpit was shot through with quick slants of incongruous light. A man from the rear compartment appeared beside Tom Stafford with about a dozen photos sealed in plastic sleeves. The photos were of the general in space suits, holding under his arm helmets shaped like fish bowls. He stood with the comrades with whom he had rocketed away from the earth, in front of Saturn V rockets or crisp American flags. Stafford dutifully inscribed and signed each photo. The man frowned closely at each picture, and blew away any dust that might have alighted during its brief exposure to air; he carefully replaced each picture in its plastic sleeve and then disappeared as quietly as he had come.

As we neared Guam a flight attendant asked me to hand over my flowers. I refused at first. They were from Thailand. The attendant was politely adamant. It is illegal to bring plants from a foreign country into a territory of the United States. When I surrendered the garland, she dropped it into a plastic trash bag. Laura patted me on the arm. "It's all right," she said. "Don't worry about it." A second attendant moved quickly toward the rear of the plane, spraying side to side with a sweet-smelling pesticide.

On Guam, a small crowd of air force wives and children watched us land from a small, grassy area across the tarmac. Some of them had spread picnic suppers out on blankets. We filed down the gangway and onto a pair of ancient school buses. A heroically clean-cut airman bounded aboard my bus and shouted, "Welcome to Anderson Air Force Base, Guam, USA!" We cheered as if he had freed us from a foreign jail. We had traveled around the world until we reached the suburbs of America from the other side. Patriotism filled the bus like nerve gas. The hair on the back of my neck stood for the national anthem. We told our airman about the soldiers in Dubai. He smiled and shook his head. Somebody suggested he go back there with his buddies and kick some ass, just like we did in the Gulf War.

The United States Air Force got us back into the air faster than anyone else. They were seventeen seconds faster than the French. We were in the tiny waiting room at Anderson less than five minutes before a lieutenant with red hair ordered us back on the bus. She was polite but firm; she made it clear that dragging our feet was not an option. I ran across the waiting room and bought a Diet Coke simply because the vending machine took American money. I felt as if I had been away from home a long time. In the distance across the tarmac, I could see a few palm trees silhouetted against an immense, unfamiliar sky. Our airman drove us back to the Concorde. We milled around while the ground crew finished refueling the plane, and then the lieutenant ordered us back on board. The passengers in the rear compartment carried blue boarding passes, while those of us in the forward compartment held yellow. The blues always boarded first. The lieutenant wished the blues a good flight while simultaneously telling them to hurry. Only General and Mrs. Stafford were afforded deferential treatment. They left the plane first, and disappeared into a staff car with a tag on the front bearing three gold stars. When it was time to go, they boarded last. An air force base, I suppose, is probably the best place left on earth to be a retired astronaut. The women and children on the grassy area across the tarmac had not moved since we landed. They did not move as we taxied away.

Guam – Honolulu 3:20:02

A woman in the rear compartment figured out that if you draped a shirt over your head you could see the stars when you looked out the window. The window of the plane was warm against my face. The hull temperature of a Concorde can reach two hundred and forty degrees during flight. The stars lit the dome of the sky; the sky defined the black curve of the earth. The earth is not a big place. Laura and I took turns looking out the window. When we reached Hawaii a single, dim strand of streetlights marked the black edge of the ocean; a jagged, dark outcropping of volcanic rock loomed like bone behind the lights. The lights glowed like foolish ideas between the mountain and the sea. Approaching Honolulu, the streetlights ran together into sparkling, amber grids. The grids swept away from the ocean toward the mountains that surrounded the city. At the mountains they unraveled into solitary threads that twisted and climbed upward like vines. We landed at four o'clock in the morning Honolulu time, ten o'clock the same morning in New York. We once again lived inside the same day as our bodies. We were catching up with ourselves.

The guy in charge of directing the plane into the terminal waved it to a stop in the wrong place. He probably does not get much practice on third shift. The jetway coming out from the terminal did not line up with the door of the plane. Ground crew members, each one more important-looking than the one that preceded him, came to the open end of the jetway and leaned out for a look. The last guy wore a necktie. He shook his head and waved to somebody on the ground. We could not get off the plane and the caterers could not get on. The air on board quickly grew hot and close. The plane began to seem even smaller. We had begun to smell a little European. In the rear compartment, the contest winners cheerfully swapped deodorants and bottles of cologne. Laura and I somberly divided our last pack of moist towelettes. "We can't sit here for an hour waiting for these bloody idiots to screw things up," Helios said. "All we need is gas. We don't need food and pineapple."

Kyle Petty passed the time in Hawaii hunched over a Modern Library edition of *The Castle*, by Kafka. He is a third-generation NASCAR driver. He uncannily resembles his famous father, Richard Petty, although he is sleeker and more polished, like a matinee idol playing Richard Petty in a movie. I spent a lot of my early childhood pretending to be Richard Petty. I pedaled my tricycle around and around the house we lived in, roaring like the Petty Plymouth. The Petty Plymouth was the closest thing to an icon 1960s North Carolina had. One of my earliest memories is of my father taking me to see it. Richard Petty was doing a promotional appearance at Cowan Tire and Battery in Forest City, North Carolina. Promotional appearances are perhaps the curse of the Petty clan, the price they pay for living faster than everyone else. My father and I stood close enough to the car to touch it. When Petty fired up the engine, I climbed Daddy like a tree. This seemed particularly important on the ground in Hawaii at four o'clock in the morning. "Yeah," Kyle Petty said, "kids love race cars, all right. Until you crank 'em." He didn't quite seem to understand what I meant. I didn't quite understand what I meant.

Honolulu – Acapulco 3:24:21

The Coors Light Concorde had begun to smell like the freshman locker room at my high school, where taking your gym clothes home to be washed was considered a sign of weakness. Hawaii had taken away whatever pretensions of personal hygiene we might have had left. Laura wriggled her nose somewhere over the Pacific and said, "Is that one of us?" I told her I couldn't tell anymore.

The one hour and forty-seven minutes we spent on the ground in Honolulu had been our longest stop. We had spent almost that long on the ground in Bangkok, but in Bangkok we had been given flowers. In Hawaii not even the rumored environmental protest of our trip had materialized. The cleaning crew had been stranded on the tarmac along with the caterers. The rest rooms on board would not have been out of place in an interstate service station. The attendants in their tuxedos and Nina Ricci uniforms bravely dived into the rest rooms and cleaned them as best they could. When we took off, at dawn, Diamond Head was obscured by rain clouds. The good news was that despite the delay and hardship we were still one hour and two minutes ahead of schedule. "If the Mexicans don't screw up," Helios said, "we've got it made."

A Concorde with no food on board rapidly becomes just another cramped airplane. I tried not to complain about being hungry because it seemed like a particularly disingenuous thing to do. Laura and I had passed on the light breakfast served between Guam and Honolulu because we had heard that a luau awaited us at the airport. Before Hawaii, we had talked a lot about hunger and suffering and injustice. It had seemed like the thing to do while looking down on the curvature of the earth from Row 3 of a Concorde; it made us feel better while we waved away exotic cheeses. But after missing two meals, the problems of five billion strangers did not seem so weighty. Let them eat cake. I began drinking Coors Lights for the carbohydrates they contained. Hunger made the marketing guys even randier than usual. Caroline, our flight attendant for the last several legs of the flight, spilled a drop of champagne onto the crotch of the marketing guy across the aisle. He said, "Sweetheart, I need you to wipe that up."

She said, "It's *champagne. Champagne* does not stain."

Acapulco was surrounded by a furrowed range of steep, green mountains. Large, white villas perched on the sides of the mountains peered out toward the sea. The runway lay on a narrow strip of land between a still bay and the open Pacific. It did not seem long enough to entice even the smallest plane into landing. Caroline cheerfully told us it was much too short for a Concorde. We banked hard left and I looked straight down into the white lines of the surf rising up out of the ocean. The surf ran up onto a beach strewn with people laid out on bright squares of cloth, like casualties in an exploded Matisse. In the lowlands around the airport, thousands of palm trees had been planted in rows as precise as the lines on graph paper. A thick, low jungle grew up in the perfect squares lined off by the palms. The green jungle was as bright as neon beneath the tropical sun. Looking at Mexico almost hurt my eyes. We came in steeply and braked hard. The runway turned out to be long enough.

We walked off the plane and into a party. An eight-piece mariachi band awaited us in our private lounge. Paper lanterns and streamers hung from the ceiling. The men in the band played trumpets and strummed big guitars and sang romantic Mexican folk songs in quavering voices. They wore tight pants and short jackets and cowboy boots. On their heads sat immense sombreros, the kind you might win shooting free throws at an amusement park in Pennsylvania. Six teenage girls in native costume performed a traditional Mexican dance. They might have been the same girls who had danced on the strewn flower petals in Thailand. They might have been clogging in gingham dresses at a ribbon-cutting in North Carolina. *Wherever you go in the world, teenage girls will dance when you get there.* This small revelation flooded me with the same vague, sentimental hope that makes me want to cry for about two weeks every year at Christmas.

At the back of the room, a long banquet table was covered with steaming dishes of Mexican food, compliments of Air France. I asked Randy if he knew how to speak Spanish. I wanted someone to ask if the tomatoes in the salsa were safe to eat. Randy said, "I know how to say 'Whoo-weee.'" That seemed endorsement enough. When we returned to the plane we found it guarded by soldiers carrying automatic weapons. Randy draped his arm over the shoulder of one of the soldiers while Mike took his picture. Then Mike stood beside the soldier and Randy took Mike's picture. The soldier looked like he should have been in junior high school. He tried to glower fiercely, but mostly just looked hurt.

Acapulco – New York 2:42:04

Shortly after takeoff Helios announced that we had the record sewed up. Ours would be the fastest time recorded for a trip around the world, eastbound or westbound, by well over an hour. Tom Stafford stood in the aisle at the news and did a creditable version of the Twist. He kissed his wife several times. She was as pretty and blonde as you would expect the wife of an astronaut to be. Stafford still looked like the astronaut in the old photos. He was thin the way a cable holding up a bridge is thin. His blue eyes seemed to reflect the sky; they beamed out at the world his astronaut's confidence. If the entire flight crew of the Concorde had mysteriously dropped dead, Tom Stafford looked like a man who could have dropped down into the pilot's seat and brought that baby home. Mrs. Stafford gazed up at him adoringly. Helios was fond of saying that no human being has ever traveled faster, in *anything*, than Stafford. During reentry into the earth's atmosphere, Apollo X reached a velocity of 24,791.4 miles per hour. Stafford clicked the numbers off without having to think about them. He is writing his autobiography. It is called *Higher and Faster*.

When I was in the second grade, the student body of my elementary school assembled in the auditorium every time NASA launched a space shot. Someone prayed to God for the safety of the astronauts, and then we all sat hushed and still and watched the countdown and launch on a small television set placed atop a metal cart in the middle of the stage. During one launch, while the ascending Saturn V skipped across the surface of the television screen like a small water bug, pushing behind it a wake of white smoke, I looked out one of the tall windows of the auditorium and saw a jet trail cutting across the sky. I was sure the jet trail I saw belonged to the rocket streaking away from the earth. I stood and pointed. "Look!" I shouted. "Look! There it is!" It seemed particularly important that I tell Stafford this as we rocketed through the low outskirts of space toward aviation history. "I just thank God that I was there at that time and place," Stafford said. "A space shot was a three-billion dollar investment," he said, modeling an Apollo joystick with his right hand, "and I had the whole thing right *there*."

We flew politely across Mexico and blasted out over the Gulf. We rounded the southern tip of Florida, turned northeast and headed up the eastern seaboard toward home. Portside, Florida was obscured by thunderheads, but Grand Bahama Island spread out to starboard like a wide, green slick on the blue Caribbean sea. Throughout the flight passengers in the rear compartment had passed around for signing the books detailing the history of the Concorde they had been given before the flight. Now that our adventure was almost over, the books came in a flood, up one side of the plane and back down the other, like high school annuals on the last day of school. Word had spread that passengers were allowed in the cockpit for a look, as long as they didn't say anything, and soon a line spread through the galley and into the forward compartment. The pilots sat with their arms crossed, as if bored, in front of a small windshield and an immense display of instruments. The flight engineer looked up disinterestedly from his console when you ducked through the door.

Somewhere off the coast of North Carolina, the Coors guys

began trying, with a belated, corporate delirium, to claim the flight for their company. They huddled together like athletes and chanted, "Coors! Coors! Coors!" One of them seized control of the PA system and tried without success to lead us in a sing-along of the jingle from the Coors Light Tap the Rockies ad campaign. "Tap your feet!" he bellowed to his indifferent audience. "That's the spirit!" During the flight the eighty passengers on board had consumed two hundred and eighty-six cans of Coors Light and eighty-two bottles of champagne. One of the marketing guys staggered tenderly down the aisle of the forward compartment and addressed each of his comrades in the slurred, loving tongue that men deep in their cups reserve for expressing brotherhood to other men.

At 6:35 P.M., Helios squeezed himself into the tiny rest room and emerged several minutes later wearing a clean shirt. The sun burned like a new star in the violet sky just off our wing tip. It rose above us in a spectacular false morning when the plane began to descend. We dropped below the speed of sound for the last time at 6:57. We were lost for a moment in a bank of clouds, and then below us a barrier island stretched itself like a rope between the mainland and the sea. Manhattan floated up out of the haze in the distance to the west, connected to the world we had just circled by the Brooklyn Bridge. The Statue of Liberty pointed up at us when we passed overhead. The flight attendants shooed the documentary film crew back into their seats for the landing. We touched down at 7:17 P.M. We had traveled around the planet in thirty-one hours, twenty-seven minutes, and forty-nine seconds. We beat the old record by one hour, twenty-one minutes. Only astronauts had traveled faster around the earth. Outside the terminal, the director of the documentary film crew had us reenact the moment of landing. The marketing guys yelled wildly. The Coors guys waved their Coors baseball caps above their heads and held cans of Coors Light up in the air.

"Good-bye," Caroline said over the PA when the cheering had died away. "And again, Bravo."

Back to Earth

In the corridor on the way to customs, one of the Coors guys tried to corral enough passengers to sing "It's a Small World, After All" for the documentary film crew, but apparently only he knew the words. Marketing guys and passengers and reporters raced past him like commuters passing a beggar. In customs I asked the officer who waited on me if she would stamp my passport. She shook her head patiently and handed it back to me. "Honey," she said, "You're a citizen of the United *States*. We don't stamp our *own*."

Once through customs, we were met by a large crowd, which I thought at first was waiting for us. Instead, I found

out, the crowd was simply waiting. We were in the main in-
ternational arrivals terminal at JFK. Hundreds of people
pressed forward against the barricades and looked at us simply because there was nothing else to look at. A throng of
journalists, most of them from European newspapers and television networks, clamored for interviews as the passengers
came into the terminal. I told a television reporter that Randy
was unfailingly colorful. He should interview Randy.

Randy stepped up to the microphones and thanked Air
France and the Coors Brewing Company for being such good
hosts. He said we'd had a real nice time.

He stepped out of the lights. I said, "That's it?"

Randy shrugged.

"That was the most boring interview I've ever heard,"
I said.

He looked hurt. "What did you want me to say?" he said.

"Leave him alone," the television reporter said. "He
did OK."

"You did OK," he said to Randy.

"What did you want me to say?" Randy said.

"I don't know," I said.

Outside the terminal we boarded a pair of buses for the
short trip back to our hotel. I leaned forward and told the
driver that we had just set a speed record for traveling around
the world.

"Look at him," a passenger said. "He doesn't care."

"This is New York," the bus driver said. "You've got to tell me *something*."

Back at the hotel, I watched CNN until I couldn't stay awake, without seeing a story about the flight. The next morning, Helios was ebullient. "This is huge," he said. "Reuters is bannering us all over Europe." I called my mother in North Carolina. She had been watching CNN for two days. She had not seen the flight mentioned. I bought a *USA Today*, which gave it six lines in a newsbriefs column on page three.

Nobody in America seemed to care very much. Maybe it was because the whole adventure seemed bathed in a 1970s glow. We had set out after a spot in the *Guinness Book of World Records* in an airplane that was seventeen years old. We took an Apollo astronaut with us. Or maybe nobody cared very much because the record was not a triumph of daring or will, but of logistics. The outcome was never really in doubt. The six three-and-a-half-hour flights made by the Coors Light Concorde were not an unreasonable request to make of a commercial airliner; the only envelopes pushed in this story went across Helios's desk long before the plane ever left the ground.

By the time I got to the farewell breakfast the next morning, most of the contest winners had gone back to their rooms to pack. The hotel staff was clearing the tables. Kyle Petty had left for New Orleans. There wasn't a Coors guy in sight. Tom Stafford sat at a table autographing photos of himself in a space suit. Helios soaked up what little glow was left in the almost empty room. "It's been a kick doing this thing single-handedly," he said. "It just shows what you can do out of a home office." Laura introduced me to her real husband. He gave me his watch. She had told him how disappointed I was when I couldn't buy one in Dubai.

Mike told me he doubted he would ever fly again. He couldn't imagine where else he would go. When I started to leave he asked me to sign his shoes. I looked down. People had written their names all over his sneakers. "Why not?" he said. "Hey, twelve bucks, who cares? I'm only going to wear them on special occasions."

I rode the elevator down to the hotel office with Helios to get a copy of the official times. Now that his charters hold both the eastbound and westbound speed records, he said he wants to take a Concorde around the world north-south, over both poles. All he needs to do is figure out how to get permission to land and refuel in Antarctica. The runway there is long enough, but the paperwork will be tough. "*That* would be something," he said. "No, forget about it. It's impossible."

On the overbooked commercial flight back to Pittsburgh, I got the last seat on the plane. Three guys in the waiting room cursed when my name was called. My seat was the one without a window in the back corner by the john. I had never noticed before how little oxygen American planes had in the cabin. When I asked the flight attendant if I could have the whole can of Diet Coke, instead of just the little cup, she handed it to me and said, "I don't care."

But Sarah was waving from beside our car when I walked out of the terminal. Our two dogs stood with their feet on the back of the front seat, watching intently. They seemed filled with joy when I climbed into the passenger side of the car, as if they couldn't believe their good fortune. Sarah leaned over and gave me a kiss. "Tell me about it," she said, once we got going.

"Well," I said. "It was fun. It was very interesting."

She said, "That's it?"

I said, "What do you want me to say?"

We were headed home—an old house in a gray steel town north of Pittsburgh that didn't make steel anymore. It was a long way from North Carolina. It was where I had wanted to die, but didn't; where I had shoveled snow twenty-seven times the first three months I lived there; where Sarah and I had survived our first year of marriage, bought our first house, raised our first puppies into our first dogs, made our first friends independent of the people each of us had known in our unmarried lives. Ten miles in the sky, traveling twice the speed of sound, I had come to realize that it was also the place

I would fly all the way around the world to get back to, that I had begun traveling toward it the instant I had flown away. For the moment that seemed like enough. For the moment that seemed like plenty. We drove down off of the bluff overlooking the Ohio, crossed the tall, green bridge, and drove into the middle of downtown. It looked as if I had never left.